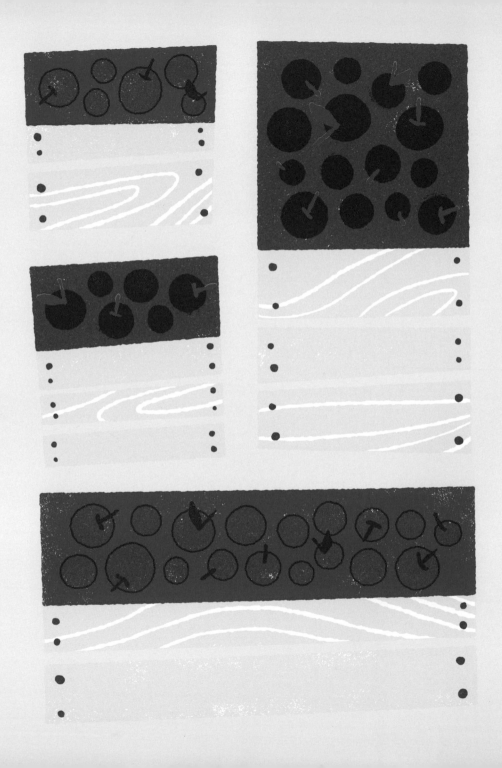

CIDER MADE SIMPLE

CIDER MADE SIMPLE

All About Your New Favorite Drink

JEFF ALWORTH

ILLUSTRATIONS BY
LYDIA NICHOLS

CHRONICLE BOOKS

SAN FRANCISCO

For Sally, for everything.

Text copyright © 2015 by Jeff Alworth.
Illustrations copyright © 2015 by Chronicle Books LLC.

Library of Congress Cataloging-in-Publication Data:
Alworth, Jeff.
  Cider made simple : all about your new favorite drink / Jeff
Alworth ; Illustrations by Lydia Nichols.
     pages cm
  Includes bibliographical references and index.
  ISBN 978-1-4521-3445-1
1. Cider. I. Title.
 TP563.A62 2015
 663'.63—dc23
                          2014038357

Manufactured in China

Designed by Ryan Hayes

10 9 8 7 6 5 4 3 2 1

Chronicle Books LLC
680 Second Street
San Francisco, California 94107
www.chroniclebooks.com

CONTENTS

CIDER BASICS:
DON'T CALL
IT HARD

How simple and natural, how *elemental* is cider? This is how you make it: liberate the juice from the fruit. That's it—cider makes itself.

In fact, anyone with an apple tree knows you don't even have to liberate the juice. I've watched it happen in my front yard. In the late summer, tart little seedling apples begin to make a carpet under the gnarled tree out there. A scent rises from them, heady and sharp. This is an ancient aroma, and for millions of years, creatures like me have been drawn to it. On each of my apples' stippled red skins is a film of natural yeast, and every time this protective coating tears or ruptures—thanks to the violence brought by insects and gravity— millions of tiny creatures pour in to snack on the sugars inside and work their fermentation magic.

In the United States, we're a little confused about what cider is. We think of it as that sweet, cloudy stuff that comes in large glass jugs. Thanks to Prohibition, Americans developed a taste for what should properly be called sweet cider, which is really just apple juice. Once temperance kicked in, farmers began selling the juice from their orchards immediately after pressing and it became a seasonal treat. In the centuries before that, they would let the juice rest in casks and naturally ferment, preserving their bounty to be con- sumed slowly, over the cold winter months—a fermented beverage everyone else in the world calls cider (or *cidre* [French], *sagardoa* [Basque], or *sidra* [Spanish]).

In the United States, fermented cider is often called "hard," a designation that carries two separate judgments. If "cider" is the sweet stuff and "hard cider" the fermented, our naming schemes suggest that the sweet juice is the natural, unqualified state. But any- one who has allowed a jug of farm-fresh juice to sit too long in their fridge knows this isn't true. In New England, where my wife grew up drinking sweet cider in mid-autumn, jugs are emptied speedily, lest the cider develop a spiky, tingling quality usually described as "off." Cider is the final state, the *completed* state; juice is an embryonic phase early in a natural process.

Don't call it "hard." Fermented apple juice is cider, just cider.

Why Apples?

If fruit naturally transforms itself into alcohol, why do people make cider from apples? The reason has to do with all the stuff that doesn't ferment. Sugar becomes alcohol, but what gives good fruit wines their flavor and balance are other compounds, particularly acids and tannins. Grapes have them, as do pears (which can be made into a cider-like drink called perry), but not strawberries or lychees. Indeed, unlike sweet eating fruits such as cherries, peaches, and oranges, apples come in different types that accentuate these qualities: sweet eating apples like Red Delicious, tart apples like Granny Smith, and bitter apples used only in cider— with names like Yarlington Mill, Michelin, and Frequin Rouge. Other apples may be used to round out a cider by adding aroma or other flavor notes, especially those tart ones, but the most complex ciders begin with bitter apples. Except for the grape, no fruit takes to fermentation so well as the humble apple.

Blended together and fermented, these different apple varieties have the capacity to produce a beverage that is crisp and complex, full of flavors we never associate with the fresh fruit: pepper, lemon, elderflower, cedar, and soil. A cider may be delicate and vinous or have a touch of funkiness with flavors like cheese, vinegar, or Band-Aid.

The Holy Trinity: Acid, Tannin, and Sweetness

To the extent philosophers have deigned to direct their attention to the aesthetics of flavor (yes, there are such people), their gaze has settled on wine, not cider. They use words like "hitherto" and focus on elements like "expressiveness" as the key to vinous aesthetics. Cider contains many of the same elements wine does, but I would argue for a more grounded basis for judgment: Balance. Humans love flavor—our prefrontal cortex developed to appreciate it—and we can fall into a sensual frenzy over tastes as seemingly offensive as pungent fish eggs, fiery habaneros, or stinky cheese. What we look for in any food or drink, no matter how potent any single quality, is balance—the harmony of contrasting or complementary flavors. The most prized foods and drinks are those that use layers of flavor together to create a single, lush impression, like a note sung by a choir.

In cider, this balance is achieved with acidity, tannins, and sweetness. A cider doesn't have to contain all three nor must they be present in equal intensity. But to create a complexity of the palate (enough flavor) on the one hand yet avoiding falling into imbalance (too much flavor), these basic elements must create a structure for the cider.

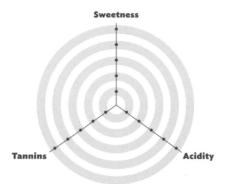

ACIDITY

Apples get their tart zip from malic acid. All ciders need acid to create a sense of crisp liveliness; acids brighten flavor and provide a sense of mouthfeel. Without acid, a cider will taste dull and "flabby." Some ciders, like English scrumpy and those made in Spain, develop additional acid during fermentation. In terms of balancing cider, acid cuts through sugar and heightens tannin.

TANNINS

In chemical terms, tannins are polyphenols and associated phenolic acids, but to the tongue they are the quality of bitterness and astringency of a kind found in oversteeped tea. Tannins also give the impression of dryness. Many ciders are low in tannins, but they can help provide a contrasting depth in the way hops offset malt in beer.

SWEETNESS

The final element is often one of the least assertive. Because sugars get converted to alcohol, many ciders have few remaining sugars. They provide a sense of fullness that buffers acid, alcohol, and tannin. The sense of sweetness may also derive from fermentation or be subtly suggested by other aroma or flavor compounds in the apple.

Further Layers

Sweetness, acidity, and tannins are but the skeleton of a cider—to appreciate the fullness of its palate, we must look at the seductive curves of its flesh—the flavors, aromas, and textures that give cider its sensual delights. When you put your nose over the rim of a glass and snuffle, you may inhale the aroma of a forest floor, full of mushrooms and cedar boughs, or perhaps something brighter, more like an ocean breeze filtered through a lemon grove. Cider is made of apples, but it doesn't always taste like apple, and rarely *only* like apples. Beyond its flavor and taste, ciders may be coruscating and brilliant, cloudy and still, thin as rainwater or full as a jammy Cabernet. Here are three further qualities key to distinguishing ciders.

EFFERVESCENCE

Grocery-store cider, which makers have positioned as an alternative to beer, tends to have a lager-like level of carbonation. But ciders may be made completely still, like most wines, or with huge effervescence, like champagne. Still ciders seem rounder and more sweet while fizzy ones are brighter and sharper. Even the quality of effervescence can change the profile—artificially carbonated ciders have larger bubbles that spring more readily to the surface while naturally carbonated ciders have a silkier quality.

FULLNESS

All fermented beverages run a continuum from the sweet and wet to the thin and dry. It's a measure of "attenuation"—that is, the degree to which available sugars have been turned into alcohol. When a cider has more residual sugars left over (or sometimes, added back in), it will seem fuller or more viscous on the tongue. When those sugars have been converted to alcohol, the body is thinner, the finish drier.

ALCOHOL

Apples have wide variability in terms of the amount of sugar they contain, and consequently, the alcohol percentage varies in the resulting cider. Production method can play a role in this, too. The keeved ciders of Normandy can be as low as 3 percent alcohol by volume, while some English and American artisanal ciders may range up toward 10 percent. Alcohol itself doesn't have much of a flavor, but it contributes a volatile, warming note that strongly affects the perception of a cider.

The Subtle Qualities

In assessing a cider, it may well be the most subtle qualities that push an average example into excellence. A cider may exhibit fine balance and structure, have appropriate effervescence and fullness, but nevertheless fail to delight. A cider becomes distinctive when relatively minor notes add layers of complexity to the final product. These are the results of the apple varieties and fruit terroir (regional environmental factors), the cider-maker's skill and technique, and products of fermentation and aging. They are that ineffable quality that makes certain ciders exceptional. Following are a few examples—but the list could double or triple with ease.

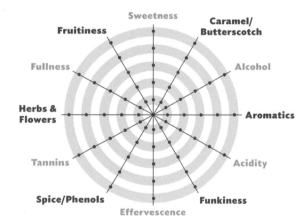

AROMATICS

A number of things contribute to aromas, but the quality and type of the fruit and fermentation characteristics are primary. Together, they are capable of producing a surprising range of scents, from flowers to fruit to cheese. You may also detect mushrooms, caramel, or nuts—or any number of a thousand different subtle smells.

Beware, however, the pure note of fresh apple, especially if it wafts through the room; some mass-market ciders use aroma distillates to goose the nose and mask otherwise insipid cider.

FRUITINESS

Made from apples, cider *should* taste fruity, right? Sort of. Think of wine and how it may have a touch of grape in the palate but mainly reminds you more of other fruit. Cider is just the same. One of the agents of fruitiness is actually not the apple, but a product of fermentation called an "ester." In ciders you may find fruit flavors that remind you of the citrus family, others in the stone fruit family, or still others that are berry-like. Other elements of the cider will enhance these qualities—tartness accelerating citrus fruitiness, sweetness deepening the berry fruitiness.

FUNKINESS

Rustic farmhouse ciders are made without laboratory-pure yeast strains. Instead, cider-makers use what's already on the fruit skin. Wild yeasts make wild flavors: vinegar, cheese, barnyard. These flavors can be off-putting at first, but let your mind expand and see how they complement the other characteristics of traditional French, Spanish, and English ciders.

SPICE/PHENOLS

Another way fermentation can inflect a cider is by producing a category of compounds called "phenolics" that taste peppery and spicy. These emerge from the tannins in the fruit. In large doses, they can even suggest a clove-like or Band-Aid note, much like is found in Islay Scotch whiskies and Bavarian weizenbiers. They are most common in rustic French and English ciders.

HERBS & FLOWERS

These aromas and flavors are delicate and evanescent—they garland the edge of the palate in lacy filigree. You might detect a note of elderflower or lavender or perhaps dried hay, leaves, or a bit of rosemary.

CARAMEL/BUTTERSCOTCH

If you focus your attention on the sweet elements, you might notice they have certain qualities. Honey, perhaps, or muscovado sugar. Vanilla and caramel are common, as is a buttery sweetness, sometimes with a touch of butterscotch. Sometimes we know which compounds cause these flavors (butterscotch is the flavor of the compound diacetyl; Maillard reactions can cause caramel), but other times it's a mystery.

This is by no means an exhaustive list. There are literally hundreds of flavor and aroma compounds produced by fermenting apple juice—and these are added onto the scores that come directly from the fruit. In the depths of a simple glass of cider is a tiny universe of flavors.

Flavor Wheels of Three Ciders

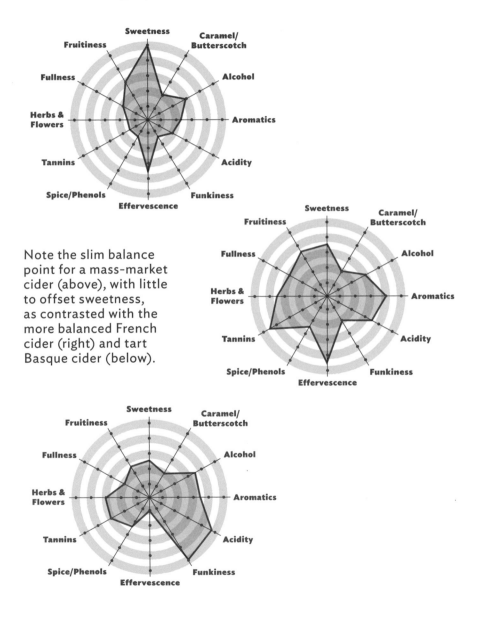

Note the slim balance point for a mass-market cider (above), with little to offset sweetness, as contrasted with the more balanced French cider (right) and tart Basque cider (below).

Reading a Label: The Taxonomy of Cider

Imagine yourself wandering the aisles of a well-appointed grocery store, finding yourself in front of, say, dairy. Standing in the soft chill of the cheese section, you assay the selection, running from gleaming toy-orange bricks to little rubble-shaped chunks with unpronounceable names. Not having a clue what washed-rind means, perhaps you reach for the safer Emmentaler, which at least includes the familiar word "Swiss." Aisle to aisle, it is much the same. Products range from mass-market to obscure. Cider is no different.

There is no single way to think about cider. If you pick up a bottle, the label may reveal its relative sweetness, nation of origin or national tradition, alcohol percentage, apple varieties, or something about how it was made. These are all slightly different dimensions that confound placing ciders in easy categories. It's perhaps clearer if you understand the dimensions independent of one another—and leave taxonomy to someone else. Let's walk through the main categories.

Cider by National Tradition

The best way to get a sense of cider's range is to find a bottle of the traditional products from France, England, and Spain (particularly the Basque Country). Cider is made all over the world, but nowhere so particularly—or *peculiarly*—as in those countries. In those bottles you'll find vivid illustrations of the way ciders are affected by both the apples they're made from and the way they're made. But remember, you need to find the traditional stuff—no Magners or Strongbow. Mass-market ciders (see "When Cider Is Not Cider," page 23) won't illustrate anything but what factory engineers can make with sugar, water, and apple juice concentrate.

ENGLAND

Cider is made all over the island, but principally in the west. Like so many things, England's cider tradition begat America's and still exerts the greatest influence on the new wave of cider-makers stateside. Americans are busy grafting Kingston Black, Yarlington Mill, Dabinett, and many other famous cider apples—famous because they've been used for decades or centuries in Great Britain. During those long centuries and all the way to the present, farmers milled, pressed, and fermented their own apples, making a rustic cider sometimes called "scrumpy" (see page 63). Traditional English cider balances sweetness with substantial tannic structure. Sometimes the tannins are so pronounced they produce flavors of Band-Aid or clove. About half are made with natural carbonation, and about half are still.

FRANCE

Cider is made in the northern regions of Brittany and Normandy, just across the English Channel from Britain's famous cider country. An easy way to understand French cider? Think wine. Normandy and Brittany are far enough north that grapes don't flourish there. Even the trees, which have to labor in the poor soil of the Pays d'Auge, don't flourish—but the hardship makes the apples more intense. The French have been making cider in these regions since the thirteenth century, and they have honed their techniques to produce exceptionally balanced products—soft, effervescent, tannic, and sweet. Cider-makers use a technique called "keeving" that stresses the yeast, leaving a lingering sweet base to their low-alcohol ciders. But the bitterness that comes from those intense apples helps create ciders as complex as any grape wine made in parts south.

SPAIN

Cider is made in two obscure regions in the north, Asturias and the Basque Country. The most exotic cider in the world, Spain's products bear a strong resemblance to the sour lambics of Brussels. Asturian cider is the more sedate of the two, with acid and sweetness balanced in relatively delicate harmony. Basque cider, by contrast, is nearly vinegar sour—a gastronomic slap across the cheek. Fermented naturally with a greater proportion of tart apples than in either England or France, Spanish ciders also have layers of "funkiness"—barnyard, cheese, and forest floor notes that come from wild yeast. Made completely still, locals use different techniques to "throw" or "break" the cider—pouring it at a great distance to rouse and aerate the subtle flavors and aromas. The tartness is a famously good companion for the salty local cuisine, where food and drink are enjoyed in lusty partnership.

These three constitute the most important expressions of the cider-making tradition brewed today. A great deal of the ciders being made in other countries at least nod in their direction, and some are explicit about their lineage. As cider-making evolves worldwide, however, there are others to keep an eye on. Germany has an ancient heritage of *Apfelwein*, centered around Frankfurt. Historically a simple product made with sweet apples, *apfelwein* is now growing up. Cider-makers are using more acidic and tannic fruit to produce sophisticated ciders that live up to their name as *weins*. North America is also in a moment of profound—pardon me—ferment, as new cideries open by the week. Modern cider-makers are taking a typically American approach. They're looking back to history and resurrecting heirloom fruit full of tannin and acid, but they're also looking forward, to the emphasis on local agriculture and artisanal production. And of course, they're looking sideways as well, borrowing from the craft-brewing movement to invent new products using hops, spices, and other fruits.

Cider by Sweetness

Left to gorge on its own, yeast will gobble up nearly all the sugars available in apple juice. That leaves a cider both thinner of body and "drier"—lacking any residual sweetness. But cider-makers have certain techniques to prevent yeasts from eating up all the sugar, leaving their products with different levels of sweetness. These are expressed as dry, semidry (or –sweet), and sweet (or in France, *brut*, *demi-sec*, and *doux*). Often, two ciders will be identical except for levels of unfermented apple juice.

Natural Cider

One category to be aware of is known as "natural cider," though it's as much a philosophy as a strict type of cider. In England, France, and Spain, traditional cider-makers usually hew to style that involves as little interference as possible. This means, primarily, that they don't pitch any yeast. Once the juice is pressed, the cider-maker puts it in a tank with ambient temperatures and lets it ferment on its own. Some cider-makers believe you shouldn't do *anything*—no artificial cooling, no sulfites, no artificial carbonation. Those are more matters of philosophy than craft, but at the very least, natural cider will have been made with wild, or natural, yeast.

Cider's Close Kin

Finally, we need to mention a few of cider's cousins and uncles. These products are closely related to traditional cider, but involve different processes or different fruit. In every case, the maker producing these products also makes regular ciders, and in some cases, these products start with them.

PERRY

Fermented pear juice. Like cider apples, certain varieties of pears are grown for perry to add a balance of acidity, tannin, and sugars. Perry is a traditional drink in both England and France (where it's called *poiré*), but it's harder to make than cider. Perry fruit is finicky, hard to grow and harvest, and then hard to make palatable. When done well, though, perry becomes the equal of the best wines and ciders.

Pears Become Perry, Not Cider

For clarity, it's best to use "cider" only in reference to apples. Fermented pear juice is *perry*, not "pear cider." This is partly a matter of convention, but it also helps avoid confusion. Many cideries now add a small amount of other fruit to their apple ciders resulting in "cherry cider" or "apricot cider." The word *cider* indicates that the base remains apple juice. If we're not clear about the distinction between *perry* and *cider*, it becomes confusing when people talk about "pear cider"—which might indicate perry or an apple cider made with a bit of pear juice.

BRANDY/CALVADOS

If you distill beer, you get whisky. If you distill wine or cider, you get brandy. The most famous of the apple brandies come from Normandy—more precisely, the Norman *département* of Calvados. Made by gently aging brandy for a minimum of three years in oak, Calvados is a layered product that develops flavors of vanilla and cinnamon, baked apple, and even coffee and smoke. Many of the most well-regarded French ciders are made by families that consider themselves principally Calvados-makers. Brandy isn't limited to Normandy, either—cider-makers across the globe also produce their own versions.

POMMEAU

One of the most interesting creatures in the cider realm, Pommeau is made by mixing young Calvados and fresh apple juice and then aging the blend for up to three years (and a minimum of fourteen months) on oak. The finished product is about 18 percent alcohol by volume (ABV) and sweet—but combines the flavors of fresh apple and wood aging in an unexpected beverage that bears passing resemblance to dessert wines.

ICE CIDER

The most recent by far of the "traditional" ciders—it dates back only a generation—is something called ice cider (*cidre de glace*). It's produced in Quebec, mainly in the region just north of the New York and Vermont borders and south of Montreal. It began about the time of Kurt Cobain (the early 1990s), when cider-makers in the region noticed that certain varieties of apples stayed on the trees long after the leaves fell and the snows flew. Borrowing a page from the vintners who pressed frozen grapes to make ice wine, cider-makers waited until the dead of winter and pressed these apples. A heavy juice trickled out and they fermented it—thus was born this viscous treat that balances syrupy sweetness with knives of acid. Production is so far small enough, and the technique recent enough, that it hasn't become a venerated traditional product yet. But soon, very soon.

Is it perfectly clear now? Not quite? No worries—anything new can seem more complicated than it really is. Keep reading and soon it will all make perfect sense.

When Cider Is Not Cider

People coming to cider for the first time borrow from what they know of other fermented beverages—generally a useful and helpful habit. But there is one way in which cider is very different from beer and wine. Even the cheapest plonk, sold in the largest jug, is still 100 percent wine. The cheapest tin-can beer, sold exclusively in bulk, is still 100 percent beer. But cider? The amazing, disturbing fact about cider is that it is usually *not* 100 percent fermented apple juice. In fact, most supermarket ciders are made up of as much as half—65 percent in Britain—other stuff. A lot of what is being passed off as "cider" is instead a Frankenstein drink of additives and flavorings.

It started out innocently enough. Apple juice takes space; as cideries started growing and moving off the farm in the nineteenth century, they had to house ever larger facilities to store autumn-pressed juice for release throughout the year. Early industrialists hit on the idea of concentrating the juice, which substantially reduced their storage requirements. It also let them keep some of the juice aside so they could make cider year-round. When it was time to make a cider, all they had to do was hydrate, ferment, and go. And, depending on how you look at it, this was still 100 percent apple juice.

But over time, cider-makers began to cut other corners. They realized they could stretch their budget by diluting cider with sugar water. Unlike juice, which has varying amounts of fermentable sugar, pure sugar is predictable. Cider-makers learned that they could fortify their ciders and then cut them with water so that they always hit exactly the alcohol percentage they wanted. In order to meet their huge volume requirements, big cider-makers began to buy eating apples to augment their cider-apple content. By this time, Pasteur had discovered yeast, and cider-makers were no longer spending months on fermentation. They were pitching pure cultures that fermented their cider quickly—which didn't allow it to develop subtle, nuanced flavors.

Of course, after all that manipulation, the cider had very little flavor. In order to make it taste right, they had to add acids, tannins, sweeteners, colorings, aromas, and dry extracts back in. It was no longer 100 percent juice, and tasted less and less like traditional cider. As cider making entered the twentieth century, cider became an industrial product.

By mid-century, consumers' palates had adjusted to industrial flavors. The growing popularity of sugary drinks guided the food and beverage industry toward sweetness. "Cider" followed the trend and became ever more debased. In England, where things hit rock bottom in the 1970s, cider-makers produced a product called "white cider" that was the English answer to American Thunderbird—up to 10 percent alcohol, and made with as little as 25 percent apple juice. It wasn't really even gesturing toward cider anymore—it was just a quick way to catch a buzz.

Things have improved since those dark days, but the vast majority of cider on the market is not made from 100 percent juice. This might amount only to a misdemeanor if the companies were still trying to re-create a product with authentic flavor. They're not, though, and that's the actual crime. Commercial ciders more closely resemble soda than cider, with roiling, artificial carbonation, candy flavors, and a palate that ends with a soda-sweet kiss. To provide a perfumy scent, they often add a distillate of apple aroma to dose their bland concoctions. It's as if someone tried to create the flavor of fermented apple juice without the benefit of ever having tried it.

For fans of authentic, "orchard-based" cider, the worst part of the trend is that many people who begin their cider journey with a can of Strongbow end it right there. They think they don't like cider, but in fact, they haven't ever had it. In the beer and wine world, products on the low end of the spectrum are often derided as something other than beer and wine. With cider, it's actually true. Cheap beer is beer; cheap wine is wine. Cheap cider, however, is not cider. It's an apple-flavored alcoholic drink.

A IS FOR
APPLE

The ordinary apple you buy year-round at the grocery store comes from a tree known as *Malus domestica*, a member of the rose family. It is a versatile tree and can be grown in nearly any climate, and indeed is cultivated most places on Earth. The domestic cultivar is a descendant of a much older fruit, 4.5 million years in the making, and a part of the human diet for at least 8,500 years. Any plant that old and well-traveled will have a mixed genome, and the apple has a couple of major ancestors. One branch of the family goes back to the European crab apple (*Malus sylvestris*), which might surprise anyone who has encountered that walnut-size, sour fruit. It has long been a staple of wild pigs, not humans.

Another branch of the family, however, produces apples like we know them—large, round, and sweet. These are *Malus sieversii*, and the trees grow up to 50 feet [15 meters] tall, laden with fruit. Ground zero is the Kazakh city of Almaty, just north of Kyrgyzstan, west of China, and a six-hour flight from the nearest European crab. Just outside Almaty, in the foothills of the towering Tian Shan mountains, are ancient stands of pear, apricot, and apple trees. They form dense forests in those hills—the only place on Earth where that happens— so lush that in the fall, fruit forms an intoxicating carpet on the forest floor. For nearly a hundred years, botanists have suspected these to be the oldest apple trees in the world, and recent genomic studies suggest they are the closest relatives to *Malus domestica*. Researchers have studied the trees in those forests, identifying more than two dozen distinct varieties that can be considered wholly wild, and another two or three dozen that are natural, ancient hybrids of these originals. Travelers to these woods, inhaling the autumnal scents of ripe apples, have called it the Garden of Eden.

Almaty: "Father of Apples"

Before it was called Almaty, the city was known as Alma-Ata, which translates roughly into "father of apples." Unfortunately, the modern city has doubled in population since the 1960s, filling up the valley once home to the earth's first apples. Cultivated trees have been planted among the wild trees, which are dwindling, down nearly 80 percent over the same period. Botanists are busily trying to preserve the original wild species, and private groups as well as the United Nations are trying to protect remaining stands. It's a tenuous moment for a critical botanical heritage.

Many wild trees are, like the crab apple, small and unpalatable. The apple tree spends a lot of energy making large, fleshy fruit— if it can tempt a creature to carry away a small, bitter offering, so much the better. In the forests of Kazakhstan, though, the trees are in vigorous competition; large, sweet fruit is the norm. Famous Russian botanist Nikolai Vavilov visited in 1929, where he found the fruit "so superior in quality and size that they could be taken directly from [these forests] to market without anyone knowing the difference." If the modern apple owes its genetic code to multiple sources, its soul was born high up in the Tian Shan mountains.

Kazakhstan may now seem peripheral to the hum of world events, but millennia ago it was on the way to everywhere. The forests near Almaty were along the ancient trade routes, and travelers helped themselves to the fruity buffet. In time, caravans deposited seeds of the wild fruits across Asia and Europe. Soon they were replanted intentionally, beginning domestication. Empires got into the act, spreading them farther and farther out. The Persians were the first to cultivate apple trees, and when Alexander the Great came through, he took apples back to Greece. Rome followed, and when the Romans spread north throughout Europe, they took apple trees with them, all the way to England.

Heterozygosity

There's an important complication to this story—just one along the way to a nice glass of cider. It involves the way parents pass along traits to the next generation. In some cases, parents create exact copies of themselves. But in others, each offspring emerges after a spin of the genetic dial, looking more and sometimes very much less like its parents. This is the case with humans, of course, and also apples. If you plant a seed from a Fuji apple, the tree that sprouts from it will not produce Fujis. Geneticists call apples "heterozygous," a technical term that refers to the way genes express themselves.

For the aspiring gardener in ancient Persia, this posed a challenge. How do you grow those apples you've fallen in love with? The answer came in a form of cloning called *grafting*, wherein that Persian would cut a budding stem from his favorite tree and insert it into a notch in another tree. This is the only way to reproduce the same fruit, and people have been practicing it for at least three thousand years. The Egyptians and Babylonians grafted, and Roman statesman and Latin prose writer Cato the Elder described it in *De Agricultura*. "Pears and apples may be grafted during the spring," he wrote, "for fifty days at the time of the summer solstice."

It's a pretty remarkable process. When orchardists plant a new field of apples, they begin with a little twig no bigger than your thumb. This is a variety chosen for its strong roots and is in fact called "root stock." It only needs to extend up a bit before the whole (tiny) trunk will be grafted to a shoot of similar diameter from the apple the orchardist wants to grow (called scion wood). In essence, when you look out over the orderly rows of an apple orchard, you're seeing two varieties of apple trees, different at the top and bottom. Sometimes farmers want to swap out one variety of apple in an orchard for another. They don't replant the trees, they just cut back the old variety and graft on the new one—a process that produces apples far quicker than planting new trees. In this way, apple varieties can continue along for hundreds of years.

On the other hand, the heterozygosity of apples means there have always been tons of different varieties to appeal to our palates. Even in the most well-kept gardens, apples tumble to the ground or are stolen by thieves who deposit their seeds any distance away. Sprouts inevitably arise, and some of them become mature trees and some of *them*—a small percentage, but think how many apple trees there are—produce wonderful, new varieties. This is how we got Newtown Pippins and Granny Smiths and Red Delicious apples—and in fact, a great many of the apples we now fastidiously cultivate. The ability to perfectly reproduce apple varieties on the one hand while having an infinite supply of potential new varieties on the other has helped make apples beloved by humans for millennia.

Applesauce into Juice

Let's go back to the Romans. By the time they were planting apple trees in their gardens, humans had been snacking on the sweet delights for several thousand years. It seems almost inconceivable that humans wouldn't have stumbled across the joys of cider by then, unless you consider one detail. Squash a grape and juice trickles out, ready to transform itself to wine. Squash an apple and you . . . have a squashed apple. There's juice inside, but it gets trapped in the pulp, which looks more like applesauce when pressure is applied. To get juice, you need a grinder and press, technological innovations that were slow in coming.

The Romans, however, had both wonderful tech and also literacy and bureaucracy, which meant not only did they invent a workable press, but they wrote about it. In fact, they didn't invent so much

They Don't Last Forever

Nature is dynamic. Creatures feed on plants and one another, and they adapt by developing greater resources for finding food or protecting against predators. Plants that propagate through cloning are at a disadvantage; eventually old varieties of apples begin to lose the battle against pests and blight. English orchardists watched this happen in the eighteenth century, as evolved predators began to overwhelm the old generation of cider apples. Many of the current cider apples date to that time, when orchardists were breeding for replacements. Twenty-first-century orchardists have more powerful tools at their disposal in fighting this war against evolution, but eventually, some of the classic apples are likely to become unproductive and be replaced by modern descendants.

as adapt, repurposing olive presses to work with apples. These were enormous, unwieldy things that required lots of space and human-power to operate. One design was called a lever-press and functioned when a 40-ft [12-m] beam (!) was lowered onto a bed of pulp. Screw-presses, of a kind that are still in use in some European farmhouses, were also a Roman invention.

That great chronicler of all things botanical, Pliny the Elder, mentioned that by the first century A.D., Romans were making all kinds of wines, including apple wine. (They also made perry from pears.) Since they already had these ship-length presses lying around, I guess it made sense to use them for something other than just olives. There is a bit of a debate about whether the Romans were the first to make cider—maybe they were just the first to write about it—but whatever the truth, cider dates back at least two thousand years.

Many things the Romans invented—aqueducts, toilets, paved roads—were not taken up with enthusiasm by later civilizations.

Count cider among the abandoned. As the globe slid into the Dark Ages, cider seemed to vanish, remaining mostly hidden from view for the better part of a thousand years. If people were making cider, they mostly kept it to themselves. Fortunately, monks continued to cultivate apples and other crops at their quickly proliferating abbeys under Charlemagne in the late eighth and early ninth centuries. This was good, because it meant that when people started making cider again—and Charlemagne issued an edict encouraging them to do so—they had cultivated apples at hand. Written records of cider making start to appear again after this period, and cider has been refreshing us ever since.

Cider making re-emerged thereafter—most robustly in northern Spain—but remained a minor beverage compared to beer and wine. The latter was popular as far north as England, where grapes flourished until the climate permanently changed in the thirteenth century with the onset of a "mini ice age." That's when cider really came into its own (though admittedly, it was still less popular than beer and wine) and the famous cider regions in England, France, Spain, and Germany were established. The great orchards of Normandy, Herefordshire, and Asturias started spreading across the hillsides where once grapes had grown. Over the next few centuries, cider-makers refined their techniques and built better equipment, making more and more cider as they went. By the start of the seventeenth century, the English were planting apple trees in North America, starting a new continent on its love affair with apples and cider.

The Cider Coasts

If you pull out a map and look at the three classic cider-producing regions, you'll see they have something in common. They all crowd next to a sea coast. England's West Country, Normandy and Brittany in France, and the northern coast of Spain are all positioned on north or northwest coasts. Maritime climates provide a regular, gentle wash of rain throughout the year with moderate temperatures that never get too hot or too cold. Apples grow elsewhere, of course—many other places—but it's interesting that these are not just apple regions, but *cider* apple regions.

Cider-makers that I spoke with don't relate to the word *terroir*. That's an oenophile's concept and, indeed, one that may have more relevance in a drink where single grape varieties are more prized. And yet, good fruit of a particular kind is at the heart of cider, and the climates of these regions have much in common. Eating apples grow on the eastern half of the island of Great Britain, but they are mostly culinary varieties; the same is true of Germany, where eating apples have been turned into cider for centuries. What makes the coastal climates so conducive to the acidic and tannic fruit cider is known for?

If we compare the high and low temperatures of cities in this region, they all track to within a few degrees of each other. Spain is much more southerly than France and England, and during the growing season, high temperatures run 5 or 6°F warmer on average—but they are still a mild 77°F [25°C] even at their height in July. Because natural fermentation was critical to ciders until the twentieth century (and remains so among traditional cider-makers), winter temperatures are a part of this life cycle. It must be cold but not too cold—yeasts make great cider at about 45°F [7°C]. Low temperatures during the fermentation months of December through April are never more than 3°F different in Bristol, England; Lisieux, France; or Oviedo, Spain. All three regions get ample rain, ranging from 65 centimeters [25½ inches] in Lisieux to 95 centimeters [37½ inches] in Oviedo. In the United States, the pattern is repeating. The main cider regions are the Pacific Northwest, New England, Virginia, and Michigan. The weather of the Pacific

Northwest is nearly identical to that of Normandy and Hereford-shire. Virginia's climate sees greater extremes, but has similar rainfall, and New England's has yet greater extremes. Michigan is a bit of an outlier, though as cider-maker Greg Hall notes, the apple-growing region is along the west coast of Lake Michigan and has something of the maritime climate, too. (Wet, but temperatures similar to New England.)

We know that all these places grow great apple trees, but we know less about cider apples. Each region has climate different enough that it's not clear which apples will flourish. Steve Wood, of New Hampshire's Farnum Hill Ciders, says apple growing is "pretty specific expertise." He related the story of a grower who moved from New York's Hudson Valley to New Hampshire and found he couldn't grow trees there. He didn't know the ground, the climate. "I think I could grow apples in the Champlain Valley of Vermont in the clay or silt loam soils they've got there," he says. "If I went to the Hudson Valley with the gravelly stuff they've got there, I would be *lost*."

Much as happened in the fourteenth, fifteenth, and sixteenth centuries in what we now consider primo cider country, growers are experimenting with cider trees in Lebanon, New Hampshire; Dug-spur, Virginia; Salem, Oregon; and Fennville, Michigan. There's every reason to think these are great places for cider trees to flourish. But we'll only know in a decade or three *which* of the trees produce good cider apples.

After a visit to EZ Orchards in Salem, Oregon, I received an e-mail from orchardist and cider-maker Kevin Zielinski. His family has been growing apples there for eighty-six years, but are only fifteen years into the cider apple experiment. He was ruminating on the pleasures and challenges of trying to figure out which apples would make good cider on his land. "It is indeed a complicated and evolving understanding of an age-old process," he wrote. "The fact is that the fermentation of apples was pioneered by farmers, not academics." Then, almost as an afterthought, he added, "We have not yet quit the apple."

Definitely not. The story of *Malus domestica* continues to add new chapters and the plot is getting thicker by the minute.

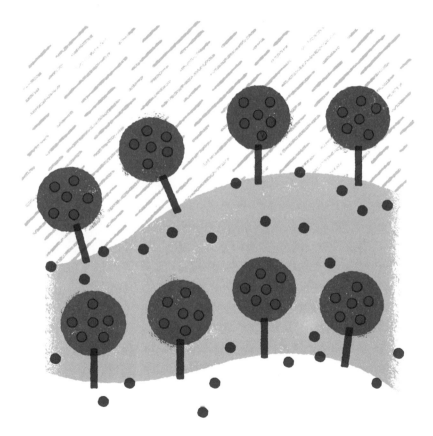

SWEATING, GRINDING, AND FERMENTING

You hold in your hand a bottle of cider, autumnal in hue, chill to the touch. You might happen to muse, "I wonder how they made it?" and imagine the answer is straightforward enough. You probably think it's made the same way, more or less, as any other bottle of cider you might heft, say at the grocery store, for closer inspection.

Well, the truth is more complicated. (By now you saw that coming, didn't you?)

There are many approaches to making cider, from the incredibly simple to the highly synthesized and many ways in between. The general contours look the same. Cider begins in the orchard; and, for farmer cider-makers, tending the trees is a year-round project. Apples are harvested in the fall and the juice pressed. Technology allows the juice to be stored or concentrated so that the next phase, fermentation, can be done either at the moment of harvest or any time throughout the year. Cideries may ferment pure juice or juice fortified with sugar; they may add ingredients to enhance flavor or not. At any given point along the process, a cidery has to choose which method to use, and by the time you add them all up, it amounts to a dazzling range of possibilities.

But among all these possible variations, four decisions in particular will shape the kind of cider being made: 1) the type of fruit; 2) whether cideries use whole fruit or a combination of fruit and sugar water; 3) the type and length of fermentation; and 4) whether flavor enhancers are used.

If we take these four markers, it's possible to collapse all ciders into three pretty discrete categories: traditional cider, craft cider, and industrial cider. Traditional cider is made largely or exclusively from cider apples, is typically fermented spontaneously, and never uses flavor enhancers. Craft cideries, especially those in the United States, make cider only from whole fruit. However, because most have access only to dessert fruit (eating and pie apples), they often add other fruit juices or even spices to the blend. Industrial cider is made from juice concentrate augmented by sugar to produce very strong, bland cider that is watered down and enhanced with various extracts and flavorings, a process known as "chaptalization" (see "Whole Fruit or 'Chaptalization,'" page 40, for more information).

Type of Fruit

Not all apples are built the same. Leaving cider aside, we know that some apples are great for eating, while others are good for pies. Flavor, aroma, consistency, texture—they all differ apple to apple. What makes for a crunchy, juicy, explosively flavorful snacking apple doesn't necessarily lend itself to a 400°F [200°C] oven. The same is true for cider.

The process of fermentation changes the chemistry of apple juice enormously. What tastes good after yeasts have had their go differs from what tastes good straight off the tree. The main elements are acids and tannins, but flavor and aromatics also play their role. In cider's long history, makers have identified a group of apples that collectively add different elements to tasty ciders. In addition, apples grown for cider making tend to be fibrous, which makes pressing easier, and have the ability to mature in storage without breaking down while starches turn to sugar. The varieties are different country to country, and their flavors contribute to the national character of English, French, Spanish, and even American ciders.

Over a century ago, the Long Ashton Research Station in Herefordshire created a way to classify apples that is still in use today. Researchers divided apples into four different categories based on their acid ("sharp") and tannin ("bitter") levels. Sharp and bittersharp apples have acid levels above 0.45 percent, while bittersharp and bittersweet apples have tannin levels above 0.2 percent. Although we often associate single varietal wines with quality, in cider, blending is the way to get the most complexity and character. Makers select different proportions of each variety for their special qualities and, in a finished cider, they become a rich harmony. There are a few varieties said to possess the acids and tannins to make a balanced cider—Kingston Black is renowned for its complexity—but no single type has as many qualities as a blend.

Following are a few famous cider apples by type.

SHARP

Newtown Pippin, Esopus Spitzenburg, Ashmead's Kernel, Hewe's Crab, Granny Smith.

BITTERSHARP

Kingston Black, Foxwhelp, Redstreak, Stoke Red, Mettais, Porter's Perfection.

BITTERSWEET

Dabinett, Yarlington Mill, Tremlett's Bitter, Chisel Jersey, Frequin Rouge, Bedan, Michelin.

SWEET

Calville Blanc d'Hiver, Sweet Coppin, Roxbury Russet, Fuji, Gala.

In shorthand, "cider apple" often refers to an apple with pronounced bitterness or sharpness, not sweet eating apples. But this is slightly misleading. Any type of apple can be used in a blend, and while sweet apples must be balanced with tannic and acid apples, they can provide important flavors and aromas.

Type and Length of Fermentation

Next to fruit, the most important contributor to a cider's flavor comes from the compounds produced during fermentation. The most profound expression comes when a cider is fermented naturally by wild yeasts and bacteria on the fruit and in the cidery. The subsequent slow fermentation, extending a few weeks to several months, is an incubator for flavor. Even when they use domesticated yeasts, though, cideries can still coax a lot of flavor from their ciders. Some craft cideries use different yeast strains for different products, and some even use different strains for different apples—which they then blend together in finished ciders. Slow fermentation is an important consideration. In warmer, faster ferments, the yeasts produce less complexity. Time is money, so letting ciders sit for months in fermentation vessels is a costlier proposition than running it through the system in a short time.

Whole Fruit or "Chaptalization"

In the nineteenth century, it occurred to a French chemist named Jean-Antoine Chaptal that he could help boost the strength of cold-weather wines by adding a bit of sugar—a practice still employed today. Although the technique is mildly controversial, it is designed not to save money but to enhance the flavor. It gives weak wine a richer texture, more alcohol, and is said to increase flavor and aroma. Governments of wine-producing regions regulate how much sugar can be added so that quality is not compromised.

In cider making, the name refers to a different practice that borrows more from beer than wine. As in wines, cider-makers add sugar, but they add a great deal; so much that they need to add water as well. It produces a super-strength cider that takes up less space to ferment, much like the related practice of "high gravity brewing" in beer making where brewers make a very strong beer

Back-Sweetening

One technique common to all types of cider making is known as "back-sweetening." Except in certain instances where yeast is deprived of nutrients, apple juice will ferment to "dry"—that is, yeast will consume all the sugars. To produce sweeter ciders, makers filter and pasteurize the finished, dry cider to remove or neutralize the yeast. Then they add sugar or juice to the cider before packaging. Because no viable yeast cells remain in the cider, the sugars won't continue to ferment inside the bottle.

and water it back down at bottling. Before packaging, the chaptalized cider is watered back down and treated with flavorings. The goal is not to increase flavor, but make it easier to manage gigantic amounts of liquid. In the United States, up to 50 percent of the cider may be made of non-apple ingredients—and almost two-thirds in the United Kingdom.

Traditional and craft cideries use whole fruit juice. A fairly reliable way to tell whether a cider is made from whole juice is to look at the alcohol percentage. Most non-French ciders will naturally have a strength of 6 percent ABV or higher. Chaptalized ciders are beer-strength at 4.5 to 5.5 percent. It's especially telling if all the ciders in a company's line have the same ABV.

Flavor Enhancers

When cideries use many varieties of acidic and tannic fruit, they have lots of flavors to work with. When they begin with dessert apples or juice concentrate—and especially when they chaptalize—they begin and end with fewer flavors. Speedy fermentations add little to the mix, and the results are bland. To add a bit of zip, cidermakers have a tool kit that includes colorings, acids (usually malic, but also citric, lactic, and tartaric), tannins, and aroma essences. These are generally natural extracts, and they are not always listed on a label.

Cider Making at a Glance

The following chapters describe in detail the philosophies and methods of traditional and craft cideries. We'll tour the orchards and cideries of Europe and North America. Ciders vary, sometimes dramatically, from region to region, and recognizing these differences is the key to understanding the essence of cider. Opposite is a brief chart that distills the process for easy reference.

Everyone has opinions about which of these methods is laudable, acceptable, or condemnable, and each person must choose to draw lines according to individual, subjective criteria. (And lest you think the scorn flows in only one direction, let me assure you that I have heard praise and contempt heaped on examples of each of these kinds of ciders.) Far more important than developing a philosophical (or worse, moral!) code regarding these different kinds of ciders, however, is *recognizing* the differences.

It makes little sense to judge supermarket cider by the standards of a funky Spanish *sidra*—they are in important ways entirely distinct beverages. Ciders are made of different fruit using different methods and they definitely taste different. You will probably develop a preference for certain styles along the way, but, more important, you'll develop the ability to distinguish type from type, and quality within a class of ciders.

	Traditional	Craft	Industrial
Harvest	Traditional cider-makers use fruit from their own orchards. The apples are cider varieties typical for the area or, in the case of U.S. makers, typical of the type of cider being made. They may use livestock in the fields, which act as natural fertilizers, and often do not treat their crops with pesticides or fertilizer.	Craft producers may maintain their own orchards, typically of dessert varieties. If they don't have their own apples, they may work with local growers and buy whole fruit, or may buy juice rather than press their own apples.	Industrial producers rely on apple juice concentrate, which they are able to buy year-round. Some cider apples may be used, but often only in small quantities; concentrate is an international commodity and can be sourced from North American, European, or Asian suppliers.
Pressing	Pressing happens at the farm throughout harvest season. Traditional makers will create rough blends with the apple varieties as they come in. Because they ferment naturally, the juice is cellared immediately.	Some craft makers press their own apples, but many have their apples pressed off-site at a commercial pressing facility. Some smaller makers share presses or rent presses from nearby wineries or cideries.	Industrial producers do not process whole fruit.
Processing	The only processing in traditional cider making is the occasional use of sulfites to assure a clean fermentation.	Some craft cider-makers use sulfites. Many add other fruit juices or spices to give more character to dessert-fruit ciders.	Ciders are made by chaptalization and augmented with flavorings, acids, tannins, and colors.
Fermentation	Fermented with ambient or wild yeasts at cool temperatures for several weeks to several months.	Fermented with pure domesticated yeast strains. May be fermented warm for several days or colder for up to a few months.	Fermented with neutral domesticated yeast at warm temperatures for a few days to a couple weeks.
Aging	Ciders are often aged until their elements come into harmony. Many traditional cideries use wooden casks to add character.	Aging is a rarity, though some cideries have small barrel programs.	Industrial ciders are not aged.
Packaging	May package still, or use natural or artificial carbonation. May or may not pasteurize.	May package still, or use natural or artificial carbonation. May or may not pasteurize.	Ciders diluted to specified levels, artificially carbonated, and pasteurized.

PROPER ENGLISH CIDER

The county of Herefordshire is one of England's most sparsely populated—a boon if one happens to be steering a Vauxhall Astra along its spacious roads. Herefordshire borders Wales, a country through which one briefly passes on the way up from Bristol, as I was one uncharacteristically sparkling day in January. Other parts of the country are more compact, the roads narrower and tangled, but in that corner of southwestern England, an American can feel a bit more comfortable behind a right-side steering wheel.

Google Maps is a confident guide, and sends one on a crisp, straight line—right up until the end. I was trying to find Mike Johnson at his Ross-on-Wye Cidery, with an address as typical for England as it was mystifying to the programmers in Mountain View: Broome Farm, Peterstow, Ross-on-Wye. No street, no number. The GPS wasn't far off, though. It sent me down a single-car lane that looked more like a miniature gorge, bordered on either side by towering hedgerows, and delivered me to the neighboring farm. An enormous white work horse was in the driveway to welcome me, and I took from his placid expression the message that Mike could be found farther down the lane.

Broome Farm is where the Johnson family has been growing apples and pears for generations. Apple trees and sheep start to appear on the downhill side of the farm, and up the drive a ways is a small herd of alpaca. The eighteenth-century farmhouse doubles as a guesthouse and, as I was soon to learn, triples as the cidery's visitor's center/cider cellar. Suitcase in tow, I found Mike there, pottering about underneath the house next to a row of wooden barrels, each containing a different type of cider. We introduced ourselves and he gestured to the casks.

"Do you fancy a tot?"

When connoisseurs rhapsodize about English farmhouse cider, they usually invoke Somerset, farther south, as the mystical center of English cider making, but Herefordshire probably has more claim. This is the home of the famous cider pioneer, Bulmers, a name now generally spat out as an insult. It wasn't always the case, though, that the world's first industrial cider-maker was associated with lowbrow stuff. And it's not incidental that the Bulmers got their start in Herefordshire: this is where the apples are.

Apples have been a part of this landscape since at least the fifteenth century and, in 1664, English intellectual and diarist John Evelyn described it as "one entire orchard." Apples were grown elsewhere in England, but more sparsely; in the east, they were grown chiefly for eating. It was in the west where cider apples were grown—in the three counties of Worcestershire, Gloucestershire, and Herefordshire, and farther south in Devon and Somerset. But of all of these, Herefordshire was king. By the end of the seventeenth century, it was producing the most cider in England—a distinction it has maintained since.

Despite the long history, cider was insensitive to industrialization. Whereas brewing had become a specialized profession more than a thousand years earlier, cider making was still done piecemeal, on the farm. It integrated perfectly into the farm life, and keeping orchards accomplished something akin to what we would now call "sustainable agriculture." Orchards gave farmers a place to graze their sheep, and the sheep kept the grassy orchard floor trim and well-fertilized. Making cider gave farmers a way to preserve their crop—and sometimes, gave them currency to pay their workers. This also meant, however, that cider making remained fragmented, seasonal, and very small scale. There were a few commercial producers, but they were dependent on the amount of fruit their orchards produced. As is still the case, farmers were not solely

Traditional English Cider

There is no particular guideline within the English tradition about whether a cider should be sweet or dry, effervescent or still. You'll find all kinds, and most cideries make a range. What does make an English cider "proper" is the fruit, which should be composed of a preponderance of tannic varieties. In Herefordshire, bittersweets make up as much as 90 percent of the blend, while Somerset will allow the use of a few more tart apples. In either case, the flavor of a traditional English cider leans heavily on lip-smacking tannins. These are exhibited best in still, dry ciders (for which most cider-makers admit a preference), which have a drying quality on the palate and a lingering bitterness. They are balanced by a subtle tartness, fruity flavors, and often just a hint of wildness that comes from natural fermentation.

orchardists—apple and pear trees were just a part of the farm's ecosystem.

Small-scale cider making has never vanished in Herefordshire, but it was mightily tested by the rise of the commercial giants like Bulmers in the 1960s. Indeed, Herefordshire can be read as a metaphor for English cider making. In the span of less than a hundred years, from the late nineteenth century through the 1980s, commercial cider overwhelmed and largely displaced farmhouse stock, and the very definition of cider changed. Even today, Bulmers is the dominant force in the county—Mike Johnson, for example, still sells the bulk of his apples to them. People now expect a different product when they order "cider" in a pub. The farmhouse products—strong, still, and full of character—are almost forgotten. Yet in the shadow of Bulmers and Weston's, small cider-makers continue to make those farmhouse products. The very existence of large cider-makers producing indifferent products seems to feed the passion of small producers and their fans. Like craft brewers of a generation ago, they exist partly as a rebuttal to commercial cider, a reminder of the true heritage of Herefordshire.

The Industrialization of Cider Making

No country is more identified with cider than England, and for good reason. The English consume more cider than any other country—about half the world's total—and of course that means they make the most, as well. Nevertheless, the state of Britain's traditional cider is dismal (though improving), largely because of the decisions made by the very industrial cider-makers who helped make England number one. Beginning in the late 1800s, a few far-sighted businessmen saw the potential of cider and harnessed technology to move it from the farm to the factory floor. A few names can take most of the dubious credit for this—Weston and Gaymer are two biggies—but none more than Fred and Percy Bulmer. They were the true kings of cider.

Although the Bulmers hailed from Herefordshire, they weren't farmers. Percy, the younger brother, was so sickly that the family didn't allow him to follow Fred off to Cambridge. Percy decided to go into business instead, and in 1887 tried his hand at cider making. Perhaps because he wasn't a farmer, Percy didn't think like a typical cider-maker. Instead, he built his business on a series of unorthodox decisions. Following two years of modest production, and now with the help of his brother, Percy took out a series of expensive loans in order to dig out a large cellar capable of holding two hundred thousand gallons of cider. The Bulmers had already experienced one of the common vagaries of cider making—a bad year for apples—and they wanted to build in aging capacity to tide them over during hard times.

The Bulmers wanted to begin using technology as soon as they had the capital to do so. They weren't the first to use steam power and hydraulic presses—that distinction goes to William Gaymer Jr., who had done it back in 1870—but they were adding steam and hydraulics by the early 1890s.

Rather than planting acres and acres of orchards for his new venture, Percy planned to buy apples rather than grow them. This was the Bulmers' great innovation. Within a few years, the brothers hit upon the revolutionary idea of contracting with farmers for their apples. It was far easier to add capacity by contracting with farmers who already had mature trees than planting new trees themselves. To this innovation they added another: In 1898, they planted a large orchard as a nursery for varieties they favored. From it they could supply scion wood to their contract farmers.

Hereford ciders of the day came in two general classes: a rough, raw grade and finer wine-like cider sold to the wealthy. The Bulmers were committed to selling only the good stuff. There may have been an element of pride-in-craft in that decision, but mostly it was shrewd business. Fine cider competed with wine (and sold for wine prices), while the rough stuff went to local pubs on the cheap. Percy Bulmer was so committed to quality that he went to France to learn how to make Champagne, techniques he brought back to Herefordshire for a cider made in the *méthode champenoise*. Bulmers later called it "Pomagne" to drive the point home (*Pom* for *pomona*, or apple, and *agne* to signal the bubbly).

For decades, Bulmers was synonymous with quality. The company received a royal warrant in 1911 (allowing them to supply the royals and advertise the fact), and cultivated the image of a luxury brand. Eventually, though, they began to reach for a wider market. In 1919, Bulmers was the first cidery to release an artificially carbonated product, though soon others followed their lead. Then, in the 1920s, as breweries were trying to recover from war rationing, cider-makers made a fateful decision. They decided to partner with breweries to increase their pub trade. Breweries, particularly in the West Country, were happy to add a popular product, and cideries thought it was a good way to expand their market.

The choice probably just seemed like a smart business decision at the time, not an existential change of course. And for a while, nothing much did change. The marriage with breweries accomplished what Bulmers hoped: selling a lot more cider. They found national distribution and saw their volumes soar. The problem was that, sold on draft in the pubs, cider started to seem more like beer than wine. Percy's old Pomagne had been slotted to compete against Bordeaux. But by the 1960s, products like Strongbow were alternatives to pints of mild and bitter ale. In the course of a few decades, the way cider was made and sold changed its nature from a product that could compete with wine on quality to one that could compete with beer on price.

To lower prices, the product was no longer slowly aged in oak and naturally fermented in corked bottles. It was made with concentrate, sugar, and colorings. For the better part of a century, Bulmers had been relying on local growers for the bulk of their juice. As production spiked, they had to be ever more concerned about supply. Until the 1970s, smaller farmhouse producers still flourished in the countryside, but Bulmers soon started aggressively purchasing them. Cider-maker Tom Oliver, whose family watched it occur, explained what happened next. "So we got to 1970, and they were the only cider-makers. They were the only ones taking fruit. Everybody was growing and selling to Bulmers and relying on Bulmers—as they still do—and the only cider you could get when you went out was Bulmers."

Once it had conquered the English market, Bulmers had to look abroad for growth. For twenty years, beginning in the early 1990s, it went on an acquisition spree—one that ultimately left the company overextended and overleveraged. In 2003, the family was forced to sell, and the suitor was, appropriately, a brewing conglomerate. By that time, cider had become fully integrated as a pub drink. Its absorption into the firmament of beer was complete.

Led by Bulmers, big makers had turned England into the world's biggest cider market. In the process, however, they transformed the product into something that only vaguely resembled the ciders Fred and Percy started out making. In beer, whisky, and wine, the pendulum has swung back from mass-market products to more flavorful, traditional beverages, and there's some evidence the trend may be visiting cider, too. But the long legacy of the Bulmers will make the transition a slow and difficult one.

Small Farms Make Great Cider

The image in people's minds of the English cider-maker involves a small farm of rolling hills, sheep under the trees, and a wooden press in the barn. Indeed, even as they were making this tableau a rarity, large cider-makers were cultivating that very image. And yet, despite being out-of-date, the fact is that good English cider—and good English cider may be the best in the world—*is* still made on small farms, not in factories. You have only to visit the Broome Farm to verify it. The reason is because it takes good fruit and a lot of patience to make good cider—qualities found in abundance on a farm.

Mike took me out behind his barn and gestured to a perry pear tree planted around 1828. He pivoted and swept his hand across a portion of the farm. "This orchard here, for example, my grandfather put some of those cider apples in in the 1930s, so we've always had cider fruit here." Mike and his father began selling cider to the public in 1984, and, in the more than thirty years since, he's learned how to work with the seasons, the orchards (each apple variety grows differently), the harvest, and the pace of the yeast that turn his crop to sparkling liquid.

The entire farm is self-contained. Throughout the spring and summer, Mike lets his sheep roam the orchards. He harvests the fruit in the fall and begins pressing it. The juice goes into fermenters in the barn and, when it has become cider in a few months, he bottles it in a building connected to the house. When people come to stay at the farmhouse, they're invited to wander the orchards and even enjoy a picnic while roaming around. Mike has made the farm a bit of a destination; in the summer, he schedules bands to play in the barn, and people come and enjoy music and Ross-on-Wye cider. It's just about exactly the romantic image people have of a cider farm.

By the standards of industrial farming, Mike's ten thousand trees amount to a "tiny" parcel, but they're more than enough to keep a small cider-maker in fruit. He has around a hundred different varieties planted, though many of those are just a tree or three. "It's just for fun," he says. "I like new varieties and trying new things out." His soil is a red sediment known as Hereford sandstone, and it's great for drainage. That can be a problem in hot summers, but lately England has been drenched by rain. Although 2012 received a deluge, it was exceeded by the winter of 2014, the wettest winter on record. When I visited, the ground was sodden and the little stream by the farm was leaving pools in the road. (In Somerset, the flat farmland was flooded, and it stretched out like an immense lake.)

Like the old seventeenth-century English cider-makers, Mike maintains a natural farm—little or no pesticides or fertilizer. The key is livestock. Keeping sheep means he lets his trees grow larger than modern orchards that are low and bushy. Pushing the canopy up allows more air flow, which he believes gives it less disease, and makes it easier to prune. The Johnsons even keep a particular breed for this purpose. "The problem is that most sheep, when they're bored, start to nibble at the bark," he explains. "But Shropshire sheep don't." For a farmer, there's a lot of upside to this system. Not only does Mike keep down pesticide and fertilizer costs (he may or may not spray minimally or use fertilizer, depending on the circumstances), but he saves on the cost of diesel a mower would use. And for all that, he has a second crop with his sheep.

Soon we would walk into the barn and I would learn how Mike made cider, but as we stood and talked at the edge of his orchard, I was already beginning to get a sense of his underlying philosophy. I was asking him something about orchard maintenance, but his answer was typical (I heard it at least three other times), "I know people worry about all these things. Of course, I've been doing it thirty years and you get an instinct." If you do things simply, the message was, problems take care of themselves.

The county of Herefordshire promotes the local industry by directing tourists along the Cider Route ("the *real* cider country," they boast), guiding them to sixteen cideries from Ross-on-Wye in the south to Wigmore in the north. About halfway up and a bit to the east is number five on the route, Oliver's Cider and Perry. The address I asked Google to decipher again included no street or address, but one interesting detail: Old Hop Kilns, Moorhouse Farm, Ocle Pychard, Herefordshire. Did you see it? Hop kilns. Until 1999, Oliver grew Fuggle, Northdown, and Target hops that were processed on the farm, in buildings now devoted to maturing cider.

Among some American cider-makers, Tom Oliver is regarded with a level of respect that borders on awe. Even though he produces only a bit more than Mike Johnson, his ciders and perries find their way to the United States, where they are snapped up with glee. He's won just about every award there is to win, and the Champion Cidermaker Cup was situated prominently in the tasting room when I visited—one of the few that had evaded him until that year. But this is what separates cider-makers from practitioners of more glamorous arts: when I pulled up in Ocle Pychard, I found a still farm veiled in mist, and a farmer in jeans and a down vest. He may be a rock star among cider-makers, but he still puts his wellies on one foot at a time.

It turns out that hops were actually not the ancient family trade—those were installed by Tom's grandfather between the wars. His great-grandfather was an orchardist. When hops became unprofitable, Tom decided to return to his roots. He began planting trees—both apple and pear—but unlike Mike Johnson, he gets most of his fruit from neighboring farms. For now, he grazes cattle and sheep on his 133 hectares [330 acres]. "I am variety fussy," he told me when I asked whether he felt at risk having to buy fruit from other growers. "It's almost more the varieties I don't want too much of. So 'round here there's stacks of Bulmers Norman, stacks of Michelin. I don't mind either, just not *all* of it. They're just boring and not great cider." Many apple varieties are biennial, and some years they don't produce much of a crop. But when you're buying apples, you don't have to worry about that. Getting the varieties he likes? So far it hasn't been a problem, though he watches the market closely for changes in availability.

The Oliver cidery is mainly a two-man operation. As we were stamping our feet in the damp air discussing apples (or anyway *I* was), Tom's collaborator arrived with the offer of warm tea. Jarek Kuzelka appeared in Ocle Pychard in 2007. He started working part-time for Tom, but was soon learning about apple varieties and fermentation. As his palate sharpened and his knowledge deepened, he became more and more valuable and now works as Tom's assistant. Soon he returned with an enormous mug of milky tea, and Tom periodically conferred with him in answering my questions. Steaming tea in hand, we began touring the cidery.

English Cider and Perry

These are good examples of the range of English ciders available in the United States.

BURROW HILL is an intensely aromatic cider redolent of apple blossoms and orchard floor. The tannins have a rough edge, but the rich flavors of cinnamon, marmalade, and plum, plus some residual sugars, offer balance.

HENNEY'S VINTAGE is a lovely, well-balanced cider with bright, slightly tropical fruit flavors and very soft tannins. Together they create an almost Earl Grey quality. Although listed as dry, it is actually medium-dry to medium.

HOGAN'S VINTAGE PERRY is silky and soft, with a fair dose of tannins and a touch of lime acidity.

OLIVER'S CLASSIC PERRY, a world classic, greets you with a light, wildflower aroma. Those floral notes resolve into rosewater and jasmine on the palate, along with an herbal undertone, mineral, and tropical fruit.

ROSS-ON-WYE MEDIUM (carbonated) is Herefordshire in a bottle: vividly aromatic, with apple blossom and orchard floor and a hint of natural yeast. The tannins are pronounced but very soft and earthy.

The Harvest

What is a good English cider? This isn't an easy question to answer, even for cider-makers. When I was in Somerset, I put it to Chris Hecks, who (along with his brother Andrew) is the sixth generation of Hecks family makers. "It should be dry," he allowed. After a pause, he elaborated. "Rounded flavor." Okay, well, Chris is an extremely laconic cider-maker.

What about Mike Johnson, who loves to talk cider? The question gives him pause, too. After considering the Kingston Black single variety he was drinking, he gave this slightly oblique response, "You must make really nice, soft ciders. My opinion is, if you're aiming to make real cider, you should be making bone-dry ciders anybody can drink." That description begins to sidle up to an answer, but remains frustratingly oblique.

Surely Tom Oliver, who is an eloquent explainer of cider, could clarify. It's "a tannin-heavy bittersweet cider," he said. "There's a nice complexity to it, and then you're going to throw in all those quirky little characteristics that can give you everything from orchard floor, appleyness, to barnyard to blue cheese." That hints at what you should expect, but as is evident from all three responses, the nature of good cider still remains a bit elusive.

Let's back up and start with the apples. In England, bittersweets are king. Whatever else you say about English cider, it must have at least a streak of bitter tannin—this is true even of many mass-market ciders. They are the mark of traditional ciders, and the most characterful examples have a huge tannic backbone. Orchards in the cider-producing west are filled with bittersweet varieties.

English Apples

As more and more American orchardists plant English cider apples, consumers are getting to know some of the more famous varieties: Kingston Black, Dabinett, Yarlington Mill, and Redstreak. But there are scores of apples out there, and some of them have absolutely fantastic names. Here's a sampling: Brown Snout, Duchess of Oldenburg, Foxwhelp, Golden Harvey, Greasy, Hangy Down, Harry Masters Jersey, Port Wine of Glastonbury, Slack Ma Girdle, Sops in Red Wine, and Tom Putt. These are not necessarily the most common, but they are certainly some of the most entertaining.

The apples start coming down from the trees in late September, and the cideries do three phases of pressing—the first in September, another in November, and a final one in December. As the apples come in, cider-makers begin a rough blend, making sure to get some sharps in with the bittersweets. They do this partly because the final blends will need to include a mixture of different types of apple for balance, but having acidic apples is also important for a healthy fermentation. Low pH juice is susceptible to pathogens, so sharps help raise it to protect against off-flavors. Tom adds 5 to 15 percent, depending on the variety, and Mike says, "We work on a system of two to three, sometimes four bittersweet to one part sharp." In Somerset, they use more sharps than Herefordshire. Chris Hecks uses roughly half and half sharps to bittersweets and was surprised to hear the ratio I'd found farther north. This difference is borne out in the flavor—Somerset cider does seem a bit more tart—but there may also be some terroir involved here, too, with sharps and bittersweets expressing different character depending on where they're grown.

I was fascinated to learn that cider-makers pick the fruit up off the ground. Sometimes they shake the tree first, sometimes they just let the apples drop. In the old days, cider-makers left the apples in piles for two or three weeks so that the juice would concentrate. Tannins act as preservatives, so they didn't worry about the apples rotting. Twenty-first-century makers don't do that anymore, but they are concerned about getting fruit that's fully ripe. "Overripe is not such a problem," Mike says, "but if it's underripe, you've got the wrong sugars to ferment." This is not just an issue about maximizing fermentable sugars. The flavor of the finished cider will be sharper with underripe apples. The tannins seem to soften with age, as well.

The Press

In every book and article you find about English cider making, there is inevitably a photo of an old wooden press. Stacks of crushed apples wrapped in fabric mesh (charmingly named "cheeses") bleed juice as they're clamped underneath a heavy wooden beam. Those photos, always gorgeous, are nevertheless misleading. Old presses exist—Tom Oliver uses one as a backup—but they are a piece of technology that cider-makers have been happy to abandon. More modern presses are quicker, easier to use, and far more efficient. Many parts of the traditional cideries look more or less like they did a century ago, but the presses gleam with modernity.

Even though it was very late in the season, I got to see a press in action at Hecks in the town of Street, Somerset. The family was finishing up the last of their pear crop, and even before I understood what they were doing, my nose told me which fruit it involved. The chilly air was filled with the pears' sweet scent, like a memory of late summer. The Hecks use a belt press, which seems typical for smaller makers. It's a slick device that grinds and presses in one continuous motion. The pears (or apples) went into a hopper above the press, and were crushed into pulp the texture of oatmeal. I was surprised

Wassail

If you have occasion to be in the West Country in January, you might investigate the ancient tradition of wassailing. (And who *wouldn't* go to England in January?) The word is actually a toast that comes from the Norse via Middle English, *wæs hœil*, meaning "be well and healthy." It is a pre-Christian rite that has certain animistic elements. This is one of those mysterious rites that Americans have a hard time understanding. Fortunately, the Hecks have been hosting a wassail in their orchards for several years, and Chris was happy to describe what happened in 2013.

"Well, there is a wassail song and all the children brought along pots and pans, which they bang together. That frightens the evil spirits away. A couple of chaps brought their shotguns down and we fire those up in the air; again, that's to ward the evil spirits away. They pour cider around the roots of the tree." (I gather this is to wake up the tree in spring.) "And to welcome the good spirits, you put toast up in the trees for the robin. I suppose he looks after the orchard."

Of course, celebrants do plenty of toasting, and they have ample supplies of cider to keep them merry.

to see that the pears were unloaded from a truck in a pile beside the press while the elder Hecks, bundled against the cold, shoveled them into the hopper. The pulp came out onto a belt and was conveyed through a series of rollers, squeezing juice out as it progressed. All the family had to do was move the pears from the truck to the press via wheelbarrow, and take the exhausted, dry pulp to a nearby bay.

In a traditional press, the pulp is placed inside trays lined with a thick piece of fabric. The fabric encloses the pulp, and the whole tray is placed on the press. There are fifteen or more of those trays in a stack, and each one has to be prepared by hand. Once the maker loads the press, he slowly compresses the stack. And of course, after the pressing, each tray has to be emptied of pulp and reloaded for the next press—a laborious and slow process. There are several modern designs, but they all speed the work, and if a cidery has the money, they seem to invest it first in a modern press.

Fermentation

One of the most indelible images from my cider travels came when I wandered into Mike Johnson's second barn, the one he uses for fermentation. It has a few windows near the roofline, but the gray English day didn't have the wattage to cut through the gloom. I was immediately greeted by slender, cylindrical, thousand-liter fermenters, and beyond them were rows of wooden barrels. But back in the darkest corner were short drums turned on end, and from their caps waved ghostly white surgical gloves, placed there to indicate the level of active fermentation. Where cider was bubbling along actively, the gloves stood at attention (giving the disturbing appearance of someone inside the drum trying to escape), and where it was tailing off, they sagged. On one glove, a joker had tied three fingers together so just one stood tall. Guess which one?

Fermentation is the most important phase of cider making, the moment when national traditions diverge and philosophies conflict. What happens while the yeasts munch on the juice's sugar goes a long way toward shaping the way a cider will taste. Yet so little is known about the process that opinions about how to ferment a cider vary sharply. Among traditional cider-makers, though, there is broad agreement: it should be natural.

None of the cider-makers I visited pitched yeast (that is to say, added domesticated yeast strains), and all were pretty adamant about the benefits of avoiding pure cultures. They believe slow, natural fermentation is critical to developing flavor compounds that give cider complexity—and cite two reasons for this belief. The first is that natural fermentation involves a mélange of yeasts and bacteria, and each contributes a little something on its own. Mike Johnson said, "The natural yeasts ferment and you know that you've got different yeasts taking over through different stages through the natural fermentation."

Researchers looking into wild fermentation agree. They've found four species resident in and on the apple that contribute to fermentation. Interestingly, *Saccharomyces cerevisiae*, the yeast used in making beer and bread, is not generally found on the apples themselves; it comes from ambient sources of the air or equipment. Those apple-borne yeasts are the first to act, and that's when they produce their range of esters and other compounds. After a few days, they've produced enough alcohol (2 to 4 percent) to send them into dormancy, and that's when the *Saccharomyces* becomes active and takes the cider through the rest of the fermentation. With the action of multiple strains, natural cider contains a more complex blend of compounds.

The second reason is time. When yeasts poke along for months, they produce more compounds than if they go on a binge and gobble up all the sugars in a matter of days. "We love it if it lasts six months," Tom Oliver says. If the yeast works slowly, "you get added complexity." The mid- and late-harvest apples take longer because the ambient temperature is lower. Those batches may start fermenting when it's 40 to 45°F [5 to 7°C] outside. That produces very sluggish activity, and the yeast may actually stop completely during cold snaps. They stir themselves when the temperature rises and continue along very slowly. The gravity (see page 89) may drop only 0.001 point a week during the cold months. As the temperature starts to warm in the spring, the last of the cider will ferment out.

Not that natural fermentation isn't without risk and trade-offs. Wild yeast is wild—and can behave accordingly, with unpredictable results. These include off-flavors like the dreaded "mouse" character that smells like the inside of a rodent cage. Many of the positive compounds that come from wild yeast can become objectionable if they are too abundant. And in some cases, certain yeasts and wild bacteria will produce acids—agreeable in small amounts—that can overwhelm a cider. Indeed, that's how you end up with apple vinegar. Depending on the type of apples and conditions, Mike will add small amounts of sulfites during fermentation to retard the growth of dangerous bacteria, but in no case more than 100 parts per million.

One of the challenges is that when the first apples begin coming in, it's still quite warm outside. That means the more aggressive wild yeasts and bacteria have a greater chance to take hold, and also all fermentation happens much more quickly. "We really pay the price for that," says Tom Oliver, who would love to have artificial cooling to adjust temperatures. The earliest harvest, in late September and early October, comes as daily highs are around 60°F [16°C] and lows are still over 50°F [10°C]. By the last harvest, lows are dipping to 40°F [4°C], which keeps the cider at a much safer temperature. The result of warmer fermentation is a less complex cider—it has fewer of the compounds that give layered flavors, and less time to mellow and harmonize.

This is a special problem for Tom, who likes to keeve (a method of fermentation described in detail in the next chapter) some of his ciders and perries. The key mechanism for keeving is a cap made up of brown material that traps CO_2. The removal of CO_2 inhibits the yeast. But warmth rouses the yeast, which will create enough bubbly

Scrumpy

Few names can evoke so many different associations as "scrumpy," a word that points *generally* to old-fashioned English cider. To some, the word conjures a substance so wholesome and good it couldn't possibly exist in this fallen world. To others, it's a foul reminder of a drink that was rough and crude and essentially undrinkable. In a way, both associations—and everything in between—may be pointing to something similar.

Tom Oliver did a pretty good job of squaring that circle for me. "I'll suggest that scrumpy is something, traditionally in the West Country, that was slightly acetic [vinegary], a robust and full-bodied cider. But I think now acetic is getting tougher for people to appreciate. The old boys, as in seventy-plus years old, they love a bit of something that burns on the way down. Nowadays most people *don't*." A strong, acetic cider that burned on the way down. Whether that evokes ambrosia or swill depends on the person doing the remembering.

Incidentally, the word still persists and it tends to mean "traditional," though whether the scrumpy in question was actually made traditionally is a different matter. Scrumpy Jack, made by Bulmers, has a touch of acid but is otherwise a standard mainstream English cider.

commotion to break up the cap, ruining the process. If the juice is warmer than about 46°F [8°C], keeving won't work well.

Cider-makers mainly ferment in steel or plastic, but they also do some barrel fermentation. Chris and Andrew Hecks had the largest selection of casks I saw, and about half their production ferments in wood. The cidery is right in the strangely named town of Street, which must be flourishing; not so long ago, the cidery was outside of town. Visitors are greeted by a cheery farm store with displays of produce, jams, honey, and vinegar. A steady stream of people arrives with large plastic jugs with the Hecks label on them. They might pick up an item or two from the shelves, but it's the shadowy area behind the racks that constitutes the principle draw.

There, a narrow passageway is filled with an array of barrels with blocky capital letters reading "perry," "Kingston Black," "Vintage Dry." One had an obscure label written in chalk—"Port Wine of Glastonbury." It turned out to be a particular type of Somerset apple. The first three casks in the line were wine-barrel size, but the next two were enormous. "They're hundred-gallons," Chris explained. "Pumpkins, they're called." He pointed to an even larger one. "These are 110, they're called pipes." In the half hour I stood with Chris in that little passageway, he filled up eight jugs of cider. On two occasions, men showed up and not a word passed between cider-maker and customer. "He always gets the Kingston Black," Chris said, smiling. If you proceed down the hallway, it opens up into a chilly chamber in the back where many more casks sit, their bellies full of fermenting cider. Some are a hundred years old.

When Chris and I were sampling his ciders, I asked if he could detect the difference between cider aged on wood or in plastic. "There is a slightly different taste. The wood does give it a nice taste, an extra flavor. The longer you leave it, the more integrated, rounder flavor [it gets]. It's a lot more work, but it's worth it."

If you want to get the most undiluted sense of English cider, a fully dry, still cider made from natural fermentation in wood is the way to go. This is cider that tastes like it did in old diarist John Evelyn's time back in the seventeenth century. This is not where the market is at the moment, but having tried these ciders, I think it's where it's headed. In the way that whisky drinkers rediscovered single malts and wine drinkers rediscovered single varietals, cider drinkers may rediscover the full flavors of barrel-aged cider. "It is a bit funkier," Tom told me, when we visited the erstwhile hophouse he now uses as a barrel room. "The apple and wild yeasts and the microflora in the barrel—when it works, it works wonderfully well." When Tom gets excited, his sentences come out in bursts, like gunfire. "There is a perception of oakiness. There's the classic bittersweet phenolics that are enhanced in this; so blue cheese, earthy. It's smoother." Chris Hecks doesn't seem to get excited, but as we sipped his Vintage Dry, I observed what looked like an expression of pleased satisfaction come across his face.

I had spoken with a number of American cider-makers before I arrived in England. As a rule, they are very fussy about managing their fermentation. A lot *can* go wrong. It was surprising to find the English cider-makers so sanguine about this phase, especially when the kind of fermentation they were practicing had so many more dangerous variables. But to a person, they found my questions amusing. They don't worry about wild yeasts; they don't worry about fermentation temperatures; they don't worry about (or even test) pH.

Of the three, Mike Johnson had the most Zen-like calm. One evening, we were sitting in his second barn—the one he uses to store bottled ciders, not the fermentation barn—gathered around a small wood stove. He again expressed amusement that anyone should spend so much time worrying about things that will take care of themselves. "I have so many visitors, so many new cider-makers, and they've done the course with [a professional instructor] and he teaches them to up the sulfites, throw in the sugar, ferment it to high alcohol, keep interfering with it and worrying about it—well, it's just not necessary." I believe we were drinking one of the whisky-barrel ciders at that point, Mike's favorites. They are limned with the flavor of Scotch or Irish whiskies and have a port-like finish. "It's fine, but they're getting more like wines than ciders." Don't tell the vintners in Bordeaux, but that wasn't a favorable comparison.

Perry

If it sometimes seems like traditional apple-based ciders are an endangered species in England, traditional pear-based perries can seem like almost mythical beasts. If you look closely at the official names of cider companies, you often see "and Perry" dangling at the end (for example, "Ross-on-Wye Cider and Perry")—but they are definitely the minority partner. Even someone as committed to perry as Tom Oliver can only manage to find enough pears to make it a quarter of his total production. The market is growing rapidly, and customers would buy much more perry if the makers could produce it. That they can't, hints at the challenges and joys that are good traditional perry.

Well-made perries are spectacular, easily the equal of cider, and sometimes its superior. (Tom Oliver recently won best in show for a perry at a national contest where they were outnumbered by ciders three to one.) Oliver's perries are elegant and finely wrought little creatures, characteristic as much for their pillowy softness as their flavor. I noticed it immediately in his bottle-conditioned Dry Perry. The word that sprang to mind was "meringue"—both for the bright flavors and mousse-like texture. Red Pear Cocktail perry has a poached-pear flavor and light delicacy. (Both completely conceal their alcohol spines.) But perries can also be made of sterner stuff. Oliver's bottle-conditioned Medium has tons of tannin, a bit of herb in the nose, and a touch of blue cheese. It's more like Mike Johnson's perries; Mike's have a sturdier farmhouse quality, with burnished tannins (they seem softer in pears than apples), more alcohol warmth, and a hint of wild yeast. Those who love smacking tannins found in English ciders would approve of them. Whether delicate and soft or big and burly, they're great perries.

To produce these excellent tipples, though, is no easy task. Perry pear trees are much larger than cider trees and take fifteen to twenty years before they begin producing regular crops. (Thus do cider-makers say, "pears for your heirs.") In the three-counties region—Worcestershire, Gloucestershire, and Herefordshire—farmers have been trying new dwarf stock to see if those will fruit more quickly. "The smaller trees?" says Oliver. "There's a few people putting in quite a decent amount. Well, they've got to five years and there's not much sign of fruit yet." Beyond that, trees are prone to pests and disease and, due to their size, are harder to harvest.

Once the trees do begin to fruit, the problems are far from done. Perry pears have a small window of ripeness; and when they come in, apples have to wait. And of course, the different varieties don't mature at the same moment, complicating pressing schedules. Pears have their own yeasts, like apples, but they are more prone to bacteriological contamination and the fermentation takes longer. On the tree or off, pears are just more bother than apples.

The pears are slightly different than apples, too. They have more sugar, so the juice has more potential alcohol strength. They also have more tannin and acid. Chris Hecks, making a face as he spoke, described them as "horrible." He continued, "You bite into one and it just *dries* your mouth out." Pears have a kind of sugar called sorbitol that doesn't ferment, so even dry perries have residual sweetness and fuller bodies. The tannins are somewhat different in kind, and there is more citric acid than in apples—and in some pears, there's more citric acid than malic acid. That also adds to the complications; the citric acid is more prone to converting to harsh acetic acid (the acid in vinegar) given the right circumstances. When all these different elements come together, you end up with a drink that is simultaneously luxurious yet delicate and complex yet approachable. Trouble is, they don't always come together.

Despite the complications, it's no wonder that orchardists and cider-makers are betting on perry's future. Pear trees may be slow and harder to grow, and perries slow and harder to make. You can't argue with the results, though. "There's a *huge* market for perry," Tom Oliver believes—"but it's a market that will just have to be patient."

Finished Cider

Most of the cider in England, even most of the traditional cider, is sparkling. Of Tom Oliver's nine ciders, only two are still. Ross-on-Wye bottles flocks of different ciders and perries, and I doubt even Mike knows the ratio of still to sparkling—but sparkling definitely holds its own. Commercial ciders are artificially carbonated, but traditional cider-makers prefer—at this point you're not going to be shocked at this word—*natural* carbonation. There is a perceptible difference, if you know what to look for. Artificial carbonation produces a rockier bead that springs more easily out of the liquid solution. Natural carbonation tends to stay more integrated into the liquid and the bubbles that do come out are smaller, giving the cider a silkier sensation in the mouth.

There are two ways to carbonate a cider naturally. The easiest is to bottle before the cider has completely finished fermenting. In that process, it will continue to ferment in the bottle, and the yeasts will produce carbon dioxide. The second method is bottle fermentation, and although it is more time consuming, it has certain advantages. In this method, the cider is allowed to ferment out completely to dry. The cider-maker then adds a bit of sugar right before bottling, and the yeasts wake up and start fermenting again. Ciders often get better with a little aging, so allowing them to go fully dry first means cider-makers can bide their time until the cider has reached the moment of perfect balance. When pressed, cider-makers are reluctant to voice a preference between still and bottle fermented (it's like choosing favorites among your children), but Mike Johnson admitted, "you can hardly beat it [bottle-conditioned] because conditioning gives it life."

Ciders are bottled dry to sweet, an effect usually achieved by adding sugar back into dry cider at bottling, followed by pasteurization. The pasteurization kills the yeast, though it also subtly affects the cider's flavor by adding a note of apple pie. The trade-off is minimal, though, and the market, even among traditional ciders, is for medium and sweet ciders. Cider-makers may even pasteurize dry ciders in case they have a little bit of sugar left for yeast to munch on—and occasionally, you'll find a tiny gasp from a bottle of dry cider that wasn't pasteurized.

On the day I arrived at Ross-on-Wye, I went to the local pub in Peterstow for lunch. It is less than two kilometers away from Mike Johnson's cidery as the Vauxhall drives, and I went with my mouth watering for the taste of draft cider. I have traveled through much of the island of Great Britain, but I had never been to the West Country before. In places like London and Suffolk and Yorkshire, a tap pouring cider is a fixture at the pubs—but always one of the national brands like Strongbow. For once, I was going to be able to find a proper cider to accompany my meal.

The Red Lion is a classic country pub, with a fire crackling merrily in the bar, exposed wood beams, and gardens outside. It was Sunday and they were serving a special farm-fresh lunch; your choice of meat plus a side of vegetables, all locally produced. But the cider? Stowford Press, a brand of Weston's, and the official cider of England Cricket—a roiling, artificially carbonated, low-alcohol product. It is a cut above Strongbow (and is a venerable Hereford institution), but just two minutes away was one of the best cider-makers in the world.

I was shocked by this. "Most pubs won't have it," Mike told me. "They'll have Weston's and Bulmers—they may even have Stella." Again, when I was farther north at Tom Oliver's, near the town of Hereford, I failed to find local cider in the pubs. "We haven't had a [cider] pub for years in Hereford. The epicenter of—well, the biggest bittersweet-apple-producing county in the world, and we haven't got ciders [at the pubs]," Tom said.

The situation is better in Somerset, which has been given a boost by the annual Glastonbury Festival, an outdoor music festival that runs for several days in June. Respected cider-maker Julian Temperley has been bringing his Cider Bus since the first show in 1970. Somerset has since become the most famous county for cider, and even in the sodden winter months one is apt to come across traditional cider at the pub. As a consequence, people have begun to associate traditional cider—like Temperley's Burrow Hill products—with Somerset. One of the county's biggest draws is a visit to Mudgley to see Roger Wilkins's farm and have a glass of his scrumpy-style cider.

But this is just the thing: For now, traditional English cider-makers are depending on the palates of Londoners or tourists to sustain their trade. There are not enough locals around who still like the robust, vivid flavors of real cider to keep their small operations afloat. This is absolutely not the case in the cider-making regions of France and Spain, where it's locals who sustain the craft. In the biggest irony of all, there are certain regions of the United States where you now find more ciders in pubs and restaurants than in England. Many of the most well-respected of the new American cider-makers have taken their cues directly from England, and they can't plant enough of the thick, lip-smacking bittersweet apples that most English cider-makers now conceal behind sugar water and additives.

The trends in beer, wine, and spirits favor the traditional makers, though, and this may be why I found a buoyant sense of promise among the cider-makers I visited. People are starting to look for flavor again. This sustains the folks like Mike Johnson, Chris Hecks, and Tom Oliver, and when you visit them they infect you with their sense of joy in traditional cider making.

Tom left me with a coda that he lives by. "I know that if people are exposed to well-made ciders, they will drink them in preference. They prefer the taste of good cider and it is more suitable for drinking with food. Our real problem is being so small, our distribution is limited. We've got to get our ciders in front of people so that when they think they want one, it's there for them to buy."

And to that end, the traditional cider-makers of England continue to make their more expensive, slow cider the way their grandfathers did, spreading the gospel one mouth at a time.

4

CIDER

UNDER
CORK

When on the hunt for cider in Normandy, world-wise travelers ignore the photography of tourist boards and travel guides. As I prepared my cider route, I gave the pictures a skeptical glance. Those "quintessential" scenes of bucolic splendor are almost always taken from a quickly disappearing countryside. In the travel material for the Calvados department of Lower Normandy, I assumed the photos of medieval-looking, half-timbered long houses with steeply pitched roofs and attic gables would be as rare as January sun-breaks. I headed off hoping to sight at least *one* prime example on my travels. (Which, of course, I would immediately photograph, perpetuating the fiction of their quintessentiality.)

In this case, the travel brochures don't exaggerate. Those amazing old farmhouses are *everywhere*. I considered pulling off the road at the sight of the first one, and when I saw another converted into a restaurant a little farther on, I stopped in for lunch. I wasn't taking any chances. As I drove on, not only did the farmhouses begin to proliferate, it actually became difficult to see any other structures. I'd been in Normandy an hour, and already I'd feasted on French food, cider, and the unbelievable local architecture.

But what the travel brochures don't mention is something even more interesting for the cider tourist. Many of the buildings were built as dwellings, but a lot of them were also built to be *pressoirs*—press-houses for making cider and Calvados (a kind of apple brandy). These old buildings, dating from the seventeenth century onward, were constructed from the material available to people then—wood, straw and mud, and thatch. According to locals, the reason they're long and narrow had to do with beam lengths. The longest beams were expensive and were used in more elegant chateaux; the farmers had access only to shorter beams, which described the full width of the building. If a farmer wanted to expand, he just added more length to one end. With sharply peaked roofs, they have attics ideal for storing harvested apples before the press, and the lower portion accommodates oaken casks of fermenting cider and aging liquor.

After my lunch, I drove straight to Glos, not far from Lisieux, to meet Cyril Zangs at his home. Guess what kind of structure it was? We spoke for a few minutes in his kitchen, and then M. Zangs showed me how the rooms were laid out. The buildings are the width of one room, so the houses are segmented—kitchen, living room, bedroom, and so on, rooms adjacent to one another running in a line.

We drove to his cidery in a nearby town, and—guess what kind of building *that* was? He brushed off my amazement—these old buildings are a dime a dozen, he said, and he was able to rent this cheaply. His cidery was an elegant one with a brick foundation and scalloped roof, and it was surrounded by wood-fenced fields, which were themselves dotted with old farmhouses of a similar vintage.

The features particular to Normandy didn't stop there. His press was parked out front. "Parked," because it was of a mobile design typical of the region. Every farmer may have made cider and Calvados, but they didn't all own their own presses. Instead, each fall, an owner of the press would drive around, farm to farm, offering his services—this was the practice for generations. Neither did most of them own their own stills. I would see a related contraption the next day in Coudray-Rabut at the Drouin cidery, but instead of a press, it was an old wheeled still that farmers would have used to turn a portion of their cider into Calvados.

It's not wrong to think of Normandy as cider country, but it's incomplete. Normandy has an apple ecosystem that begins with cider but continues on to Calvados and Pommeau, an aged blend of Calvados and apple juice. Guillaume Drouin, a third-generation cider-maker at the Christian Drouin distillery, speculates that

Cidre Bouché of France

The ciders of Normandy and Brittany are—well, they're *French*. That is to say, they are subtle and sophisticated, complex, and accomplished. Most of the traditional farmhouse ciders are made through a process that leaves them light on alcohol (2.5 to 4.5 percent), balancing rounded residual sugars with tannins. Naturally fermented, many have a touch of blue cheese as well. A new breed of cider-maker led by Cyril Zangs and Eric Bordelet takes cues from the winemakers to the south, producing stronger, drier products that find their way into the finer restaurants of Paris. French ciders are nearly always bottled sparkling, and pour from corked champagne bottles (*cidre bouché* refers to corked cider) with joyful effervescence.

just a few decades ago there were tens of thousands of farmhouse producers. "Calvados was really a farm product. Every farmer was making his own Calvados even fifty years ago." The farmers harvested their apples and made cider and later distilled it. Until very recently, in every *pressoir* in the department, farmers had stocks of fresh cider and barrels of aging Calvados. The farmers didn't think of themselves as cider-makers or distillers, they were farmers, and cider and Calvados were just part of their produce.

Once I left the Zangs cidery and was driving the roads through lush farmland, I started to think about all the half-timbered buildings I could see. How many of them had once been put to the service of the orchards? Apples and their assorted nectars are so central to this region, I almost wondered if they didn't ooze from the earth.

Northern France has been home to orchards since at least Roman times, but up until the mid-fourteenth century, it was, like the rest of France, predominantly wine country. But then the climate of Europe went through a mini ice age, and wine grapes withered in the cold. Farmers in Normandy and Brittany replaced their vines with trees, and that's when the north truly became the place of apples. Calvados came a bit later, but by the early 1600s it was established firmly enough to have its own guild. The orchards of northern France flourished and grew to be among the world's largest, and cider and Calvados became fixtures of the local scene.

Fortune played an interesting role in cider's more recent history. It received an unexpected boost in the mid-nineteenth century when the phylloxera aphid arrived to ravage French vineyards. When the wine stocks plummeted, cider stepped in. The orchards spread, and an industry was born. Researchers looked into the science of cider, and France produced a number of technical manuals—more sophisticated than the material written about wine—that are still in use today. The U.S. government commissioned a report on cider making at the turn of the twentieth century, and the author, William Alwood, reported that at the time, "France, by reason of the extent of its manufacture, is easily the leading cider country of the world."

Just at the moment cider was becoming a legitimate rival to French wine, though, fortune swung back against it. The first half of the twentieth century brought two World Wars to France, and both helped buckle cider production. During WWI, the government requisitioned alcohol to use for munitions production, dealing the first blow. The second was far graver. To Americans, Normandy isn't known for apples or native son William the Conqueror—it's known for the battlefields of the Allied invasion, which touched down on the coastal edge of cider country. And it wasn't just the Allies—wine fought its own war. As vintners got control of the aphid blight, the

Asbestos Sack Filter

One of the many scientific innovations of the late nineteenth century was the French asbestos sack filter, which, as William Alwood reported, produced a cider "clear and limpid as it goes into the cask." He described it as "a fairly closely woven asbestos sack, ten or twelve inches in diameter." The open end of the sack was tied around a tube that was placed in the cider vat and attached to a pump. The must was drawn through "the asbestos sack . . . largely freeing the [cider] from floating particles of whatever nature."

Thankfully, the asbestos sack filter is no longer in use in French cideries.

French government gave it a big boost, restricting Calvados sales and banning Pommeau. It was never likely that France would permanently eschew wine in favor of cider, but this series of setbacks settled the matter.

By midcentury, the cider boomlet was over. Wine had been restored to preeminence, and cider went back to its regional status. Where it once seemed as if cider might become organized into a proper industry, it instead fell back to the farm, where makers were small and informal. Wine is again the fuel that powers French culture, cider a mostly forgotten rival. It almost didn't go that way, though. How would the world differ if France were famous for cider instead?

I would argue that of all the world's ciders—supermarket varieties included—none have a broader appeal than the joyfully sparkling farmhouse ciders of France. Like English ciders, they're built around bitter apple varieties, but they're not bitter. Cider-makers ferment them to leave much of their sugars behind.

It results in ciders that are at once sweet and full, yet also structured and complex. Modern palates tend to like lively beverages, and they're all that. Finally, tucked in around the edges are subtle hints of their rustic origins—the fragrance of orchard floor and blue cheese, herbs and flowers, perhaps some wood or spice. They appeal equally to those who have never tasted cider and those who have spent a lifetime enjoying them.

Yet making a crowd-pleaser that both connoisseurs and neophytes admire is no easy business. My second visit was to the Christian Drouin cidery. Guillaume Drouin had wanted to take me into the orchards, but it was pouring rain, and so we'd hustled instead past them and into the new and modern open-air facility situated incongruously in the midst of old apple trees. "If you think about a traditional cider, it is made to be a problem," he said. "You put sugar, yeast, bacteria all together into the bottle and then you put a cork on it. And then you pray." He had just finished giving me a tour, and describing the cider-making process, apple to cork, seemed to leave him slightly agitated. What he was aiming for was a deliciously carefree drink, and yet getting there was like juggling knives. The grinder, press, and fermenters suddenly seemed menacing.

Drouin is a dapper man who looks younger than his thirty-six years. He has swept-back hair and wears a kind of three-quarter-length frock coat. His family is from Normandy, but his grandfather, who started the business, was not a farmer. He owned a successful fertilizer company, and in 1960 purchased a sixteen-hectare [forty-acre] farm with apple orchards. He found that selling the fruit wasn't profitable, so he decided he'd try his hand at making Calvados. Because he had other income, Christian Drouin didn't need the brandy to earn him money immediately—a rare luxury that allowed the distillery to establish an impressive reserve of aging stock over the course of two decades. "Calvados is like a bank that you have to add to every year," says his grandson. "Maybe fifteen years later you will take some money out of that project."

The company also made cider, but until Guillaume arrived, it was a secondary business. Both his grandfather and father (also named Christian) were focused on Calvados. That product starts out as cider, but good Calvados is made in the still and the cask. Cider requires different apples (and more of them) and a different balance of elements; it's the final rather than first stage of the process. Under Guillaume's direction, the name Christian Drouin has become as notable for cider as it is for Calvados.

The differences start in the orchard. Counterintuitively, Calvados begins with lower-alcohol cider. Starting with low-alcohol cider requires more concentration during distillation, and that means more complexity. To get lower-alcohol cider, Calvados requires different apples than the cider that will be bottled for consumption. In order to get the right mixture of apples for both cider and Calvados, Drouin farms twenty hectares and buys fruit from another twenty hectares on adjacent land (about one hundred acres in total). The names of some of the most important varieties rolled off his tongue: Bedan, Mettais, Binet Rouge, Saint Martin, Moulin à vent, Frequin, Rambault. Like the English cider-makers I spoke to, Drouin favors larger trees called "high stem" (*haute tige*) so they can graze cattle underneath—and like the English cider-makers, this means they don't use pesticides or fertilizers. He explains, "The cows, they love the apples. In summer, they look at the apples growing and from the end of August they start shaking the trees as much as they can. When there's a worm, when the fruit starts to perish, it's going to fall first. So the cows eat them and they cut the grass. They're very useful." He takes a similarly organic approach to harvest, waiting for the apples to fall themselves (once the cows have been relocated to a different pasture), and picking the fruit off the ground. He feels that shaking a tree once and collecting the apples all together will result in some underripe fruit. "I will go under the trees like three, four times to pick it completely."

Terroir

This region is known as the Pays d'Auge, famous not only for cider, but cheese (Pont l'Évêque and Camembert) and horses. Hills roll toward the sea to the north and the picturesque towns of Deauville and Honfleur, and their slopes are blanketed with orchards. Some of the best-known French cider-makers have trees within twenty kilometers of the town of Lisieux at the center of Pays d'Auge— Dupont, Le Père Jules, and Manoir de Grandouet, along with Zangs and Drouin.

This is France, and I couldn't help but wonder whether cider-makers thought in terms of terroir. In wine-making, "terroir" is an accepted if slippery concept. It means, roughly, the natural environment that contributes to wine—the climate, soil, and sunlight. Although cider-makers elsewhere believed these factors inflected their ciders, few regarded it with the sense of mysticism it seems to receive among wine aficionados. Guillaume Drouin isn't averse to the concept of terroir, but doesn't think it is a major factor in cider's final flavor profile. Cyril Zangs, however, makes a strong case by relaying an interesting discovery he made about the role of terroir.

Like Drouin, he wasn't particularly concerned about terroir— until his cousin approached him about a coastal orchard on the steep slopes overlooking the sea. She wondered if Zangs would be interested in using the apples in his cider. He wasn't—it was thirty-five kilometers away. Nevertheless, he visited, finding old, overgrown trees when he arrived. They were cider apples, and while they were tromping around, Zangs recognized one he knew. He plucked an apple and took a bite but was surprised by the flavor. "I tasted it as we spoke and after three bites [I realized] it is very sharp like glass." The apples from that orchard make his This Side Up cider, which has a distinctive mineral quality, a "sharpness" Zangs attributes to terroir.

"I talked with winemakers and they tell me, 'no, no, it doesn't come from the sea.' The sea may make the trees very clean, that's true. But it comes from the soil." At first, he believed this meant the rocky soil and steep slope, but when he began filling in holes in the orchard where trees had died, he discovered that it had only very shallow topsoil. But because it was such an old orchard, that topsoil had grown richer. There were wild plants and mushrooms growing throughout the orchard, and despite the shallow soil, the trees pulled their nutrients from that lush layer of life. His conclusion? "Everything happens in the earth. The terroir is not obligatory with rocks and special soil; it can also happen in the earth. You could *make* a terroir; bring the earth back to what it should be."

Wine and cider are different; wine depends on fewer grape varieties and the terroir is more evident in the expression of the fruit. Ciders are made from blends of many types of apples and this has the effect of blending away subtle elements of terroir. Nevertheless, there is a terroir of apples, and it is revealed when you try Zangs's two ciders next to each other.

French Cider

These are good examples of the range of French ciders available in the United States.

CHRISTIAN DROUIN PAYS D'AUGE is a supple cider, with earthy, herbal notes and nutty tannins balanced by silky apple flavor; the company's *Poiré* is even more silky and sweet.

CLOS DES DUCS is one of the rare Breton ciders available; it's a funky farmhouse cider with a steely tang underneath a batting of soft sweetness.

DOMAINE DUPONT CIDRE BOUCHÉ has an incredible blue cheese and orchard floor nose, lip-smacking tannins, and a round, bubbly body.

ERIC BORDELET SIDRE TENDRE is a great introduction to French cider; it is approachably sweet and effervescent, but has soft, cinnamon tannins, blue cheese, and a hint of smoke.

LES PÈRE JULES BRUT is a good example of the typical ciders of the region, rustic but approachable.

CYRIL ZANGS BRUT and **THIS SIDE UP** contrast with other French ciders. They are both quite dry and vinous, the Brut elegant, This Side Up glassy and sharp.

The Art of Défécation (Keeving)

The new Drouin cidery is located on the old farm, which is actually the site of the original cidery and distillery. In 1990, after steady growth, the family moved operations to an amazing farm in Coudray-Rabut, near Pont L'Évêque. It is made up of several half-timbered structures, and they ring a central square like petals on a daisy. One building is the old house, another the historic *pressoir* where the family currently does distillation, and other buildings are used for cask storage. Eventually these buildings were insufficient, so the Drouins moved the cider making back near the original location. It's an odd sight. We drove up to it through an old orchard in the midst of which was a half-timbered shed with thatch roofing, and out in a clearing emerged a jumble of steel surmounted by a tall roof—a cidery with no walls.

Although it is a modern facility, it has been optimized to make cider using a method that is at least four hundred years old. It is the complicated but ingenious process of making a stable bottle of cider that contains residual sugars. This challenge has forever plagued cider-makers. So long as even a few yeast cells remain in a bottle, they will reproduce and consume whatever sugar is available. That dynamic either leads to explosive bottles or dry ciders free of sugar. Modern cideries use microfiltration or pasteurization to remove or kill the yeast. Pasteurization, the process of heating the cider, may damage the flavor and aroma, and filtration is not foolproof. (Recently an American cider-maker had to recall a batch that wasn't filtered properly and led to exploding bottles.) The most elegant solution is keeving, which not only allows large amounts of sugar to remain, but suffers none of the violence done by pasteurization or filtering. The downside is that it's time consuming and difficult to pull off.

Since the sugar and yeast will remain in the cider at bottling, the cider-maker's goal is removing a third factor required to produce fermentation—nutrients. If he can effectively strip those out of the cider, the yeasts will go dormant, even with succulent molecules of fructose floating around tempting them. The process begins just after the apples have been ground but before they're pressed. The pulp is left to sit for up to a day, though Guillaume Drouin has found he gets the best results in just two to three hours. Called "maceration," this process allows the pectin to leach out of the cell walls. It also oxidizes the tannins, turning the juice dark; some cider-makers believe the process leaves the tannins "softer." Drouin is one. "The maceration transforms the structure of the tannins. If you don't macerate, you get more astringent tannins. If you macerate, you will get nearly the same structure, but it's going to be a bit smoother, rounder."

The Drouins use a press typical of wineries; a large enclosed cylinder with a membrane on the inside that slowly inflates, squeezing the juice from the pomace (skins, dry pulp, and seeds). "It's made to respect the fruit as much as possible," Drouin explained. He can set it to extract a precise amount of juice, and he prefers 65 percent. "It doesn't turn a lot, and it inflates slowly. It's made for a light extraction." Once he has the juice, he checks the temperature to ensure it's below 46°F [8°C]; if not, he runs it through a chiller to drop it to that level. Temperature is absolutely critical for *déféca-tion*—above 46°F [8°C] and it will fail.

Over the next week, the juice goes through some fascinating chemistry. Enzymes take the pectin and slowly convert it to pectic acid, which forms—well, there's no way to softball this—gelatinous blobs. Fermentation starts at the same time, but because it's so cold, the yeasts are sluggish, producing only intermittent bubbles of CO_2. Those gentle bubbles rise, pushing slimy gobbets of pectic acid up to the top of the vat. Guillaume takes over the description, "The pectins conglomerate together and this makes a heavy, solid thing than goes to the top of the tank, which we call *chapeau brun*, 'brown hat.'" The hat compacts as more and more of the pectic acid rises. Those rising globs also rob the juice of much of its nutrients, which cider-makers now realize is the key to *défécation*. It is therefore paramount that the cap not be disturbed, lest those nutrients fall back into the cider.

"When the hat is made, you have to rack the cider [move it from one tank to another]. This is very important." Guillaume monitors the *chapeau* with state-of-the-art technology—a stick he uses to probe the mass and measure its density. "You have more or less twelve hours, *maybe* twenty-four, to do this racking properly. If you do it too early, the hat is not completed and we will still have a lot of pectin left in the cider, which is not good. But if you wait too long, the hat falls down in the tank. Too late; this is not for bottling cider anymore." Fortunately for the Drouins, a collapsed hat is not a catastrophe. "The problem with the *chapeau brun*," Guillaume explains cheerily, "is that it works 90 percent of the time; 10 percent it doesn't work. Then you make Calvados."

Once Guillaume feels the process is complete, he draws the clear juice out from underneath the *chapeau brun* (certain solids also precipitate out and collect at the bottom; he's careful to leave those lees undisturbed as well). All that remains is slow fermentation, generally lasting three months or more. If the fermenting cider gets too warm, it will start to ferment too quickly, so he'll run it through the chiller to keep it below 52°F [11°C]. Fermentation is a balancing act; Drouin wants the yeast to ferment the cider to a certain point, but no further. Over the course of those three months, he repeatedly filters and racks (transfers) the cider, stripping it of most of the yeast cells. This forces the yeast to repopulate, and that in turn causes them to scrub the cider of nutrients. Regularly filtering and racking the cider also gives it more complexity because each time the yeasts repopulate, they produce more flavor and aroma compounds. By the time he's ready to bottle, the yeasts should have nearly exhausted the nutrients—just enough to turn the cider sparkling in the bottle, but not explosively so.

The Cider of Brittany

When you look at a map of France, you see two peninsulas reaching out like arms toward Great Britain. The right arm belongs to cider-making Normandy, the left to cider-making Brittany. But it was into the Armorican peninsula—Brittany—where a stream of immigrants from Wales and England made the left arm "little Britain." The Celtic language of Breton is spoken there, a tongue related to Cornish—and in fact there is a region, Cornouaille, that means "Cornwall" in French. And of course, the two regions also have cider in common.

Normandy is far more well-known for its cider (more Norman ciders are available abroad), but Brittany produces 40 percent of France's cider and has a lively collection of traditional producers. Like Normandy, the ciders of Brittany are largely made through keeving and retain the French quality of roundness and balance. Ciders from Brittany, though, are on the average stronger. A typical Norman cider rarely ranges above 5 percent ABV, but Breton ciders often do. That means they're drier, but even more characteristic is the minerality that comes from granite soils.

The first Appellation d'Origine Contrôlée (AOC)—the certification for products made in certain areas of France—given to a French cider was named for Cornouaille in Finistère, and many of the features describe typical traditional practices: pure juice, natural fermentation, and natural bottle carbonation. In applying for the appellation, cider-makers demonstrated that their practices dated at least to the nineteenth century, with orcharding dating to the sixth century and cider making to the fourteenth. The official appellation also identifies seven classic apples of Finistère (though other varieties may also be used), including Kermerrien, Marie Ménard, Douce Moën, Douce Coêtligné, and Guillevic.

As in Normandy, cider is distilled in Brittany, but the resultant brandy is known as Lambig, not Calvados. According to its AOC, Lambig must be aged four years on oak, but like Calvados, is regularly aged for decades. Brittany produces Pommeau as well, though the AOC does not stipulate a ratio of juice-to-Lambig blend; it simply must be 16 to 18 percent when bottled.

Most of the traditional cider currently made in Normandy is keeved, but it wasn't always that way. A century ago, the most highly prized cider was fermented dry, to 6 to 7 percent alcohol. Sometimes they were packaged still, sometimes carbonated—either *mousseux* (sparkling, but bottled before fermentation had finished) or bottle-conditioned in the *méthode champenoise*. One imagines those are the ciders Cyril Zangs would have prized.

Zangs originally thought he'd be a winemaker. He is from Normandy and his grandfather made ciders, but they were the keeved variety. French ciders have changed over the decades, and the stronger, drier products a hundred years ago mostly died out. The sweeter ciders didn't appeal to Zangs, who much preferred wine and left Normandy to learn how to make it. But there's something about Normandy that pulls cider-makers back (Guillaume Drouin fell back into cider's orbit after a similar vinous dalliance). For Zangs, the epiphany came when he tried one of the ciders made by François David, a giant in Norman cider making. David, who was sometimes called Le Pape du Cidre ("the Pope of Cider"), also made the low-alcohol ciders typical of the region; they were so accomplished, though, that Zangs had the first inkling of what ciders could be.

David taught Zangs how to make cider, but Cyril has gone his own way, crafting ciders in the old-fashioned manner, dry and sparkling. When I met him at his house, one of the first things announced was "I'm not doing real typical ciders." It's true. Zangs makes just two types of ciders, and they have the quality of wine about them, even down to vintage dating. One is 6 percent alcohol by volume, one 7 percent. His comment struck a note in my mind that sounded, sweet and clear, throughout our visit. I tested it against everything he told me. When I shook hands with him after my tour, just as dusk was settling on the rainy village of Glos, I understood it differently. Zangs does not make ciders like other makers scattered around Normandy; but he does make ciders one would call purely French.

Zangs is a precise man. He speaks precisely, he has a precise cider-making process, and even the gesticulations of his hands are precise, like a conductor's. On the day I visited, he was wearing a tweed driving cap and wool scarf and we chatted awhile before we drove over to his cidery. His one area of abandon seems to be the road—we rocketed through copses of trees and bounced around country lanes like race-car drivers, making the trip in half the time it would have taken me alone. He gave me a sly smile when I commented on it.

We started the tour outside the cidery, at the mobile press he uses. Zangs's press isn't an antique (it dates to the 1950s), but the technology is barely updated. Once, presses like this would have circulated among the smaller cideries, doing a day's work before moving on. They have an ingenious design that allows the workers to stay in continuous motion. There are two racks, side by side. While one side is being pressed, the other can be changed out, emptied, and loaded with fresh pulp. The racks are on a swivel, so once one is done pressing, the press goes up, the racks exchange places, and the fresh rack begins pressing while the other one is emptied out and readied again.

Zangs is incredibly fastidious about the cleanliness of his apples. He waits until they're fully ripe to harvest, and then carefully sorts and cleans them. In a given year, he'll remove up to 10 percent of them

Gravity Readings

How do you know how much alcohol you have in your cider? You do a gravity reading. This is a simple process of immersing an instrument in liquid in order to see how much dissolved sugars it contains. Water, nature's sugar-free treat, measures 1.000 on the gravity scale. Apple juice typically has a value of around 1.055. As yeasts convert the sugars to alcohol, that gravity falls. In fact, alcohol has a lower gravity than water, so if yeasts are able to consume most the sugar, the finishing or "final gravity" of a cider can be less than one. (English cider-makers report final gravities as low as 0.097.)

for defects or rot. But then, just like the Drouins, he makes his cider of a blend containing no more than 10 percent tart apples. If apple blends are one of the keys to defining national character—and they are—this is one clue to his ciders' provenance. Partly because of the way the swivel press works, he doesn't macerate his pulp. Perhaps the bigger reason is because he once tried it and "saw no difference."

He has no way to chill the cider, so the fruit that comes in early begins fermenting warmer. It's one of the trade-offs with natural cider making, and one he's learned to live with. "If you have a warm temperature, you can have a yeast that is very tough and will say to other ones, 'hey shut up, I work, I work.'" Here he was talking about the dominant strains that come in the potpourri of microorganisms. When it's warm, vigorous yeasts will outperform the weaker ones. "But when it's cold, it's difficult for her, so a lot of different yeasts work—everybody can say something."

Even though he doesn't keeve his ciders, his process is much like others in France. He racks it several times. The purpose here is different from keeved ciders, though. He's not trying to starve the yeasts of nutrients; he's slowing down fermentation. Because the cider doesn't immediately get scrubbed the way keeved cider does, nutrients continue to sustain yeasts through several rackings. Typically, Zangs racks his cider at gravities of 1.035, 1.025, 1.016, and then just before bottling. Each time he racks, it removes carbon dioxide, allowing particulates to fall, clarifying the cider. And, just to illustrate the differences between England and France, when Zangs lets his cider go all the way to "dry," this means about 1.007. Across the English Channel, dry is 1.005 or lower, and 1.007 counts as "medium."

Cider Under Cork

Eating in Normandy is both a pleasure and a snap. Most of the restaurants I visited offered three-course prix-fixe menus that highlighted local cuisine. One feature that distinguishes Norman dining is the option of cider instead of wine with your meal. (As one gauge to the relative saturation of cider, even in Normandy, a glance at the wine and cider lists is revealing. No restaurant I visited offered a choice of more than six ciders; none offered fewer than a dozen wines. Cider is more readily available in Normandy than Herefordshire, but one shouldn't leap to the impression that it has displaced *le vin*.)

If you order a bottle of cider, the waiter will arrive to serve it to you, just as he would a bottle of wine. With an economy of motion typical of experts, he will uncage a mushroom-shaped cork, remove it with a pop, and fill your glass—wine or cider, it's the same one—with a dancing, shimmering liquid. I couldn't imagine why anyone would choose wine. In my favorite meal at a little café in the coastal town of Honfleur, a bottle of Le Père Jules was the perfect match for a bowl of fish stew.

One of the hallmarks of French cider is bottle fermentation. At the grossest level, this means effervescence. That pop of the cork and the vigorous bead are what people remember about French ciders. But there's more to it than simple carbonation. When ciders ferment naturally, they continue to change chemically. The yeast continues to produce compounds and add complexity. According to the French approach, a cider isn't finished when it's ready to bottle—it goes into the bottle to finish. "You always have to imagine that it will continue to change," Guillaume Drouin explains. "Actually it shouldn't be perfect at that moment [bottling]; it should be perfect *after* the fermentation in the bottle, which completely transforms the structure again. It really affects the taste."

The process takes a long time—a bare minimum of two months. During that time, the carbon dioxide will become absorbed into the body of the cider, adding another classic French characteristic. When it's ready, that carbonation will make the cider silky, giving it a luxurious quality that regular carbonation, which is rocky and rough, can't emulate. When the French make sparkling wines, they even call this *mousse*. Cider-makers typically rest their bottles upright as they condition. If for some reason the balance of sugars, nutrients, and yeast isn't just right and the bottles overcarbonate, the gas can escape out around the cork. (Lying sideways, the rising gas couldn't escape and the bottles would explode.)

Disgorgement

Inside Cyril Zangs's cidery, the old Norman building has been divided into two rooms. If you don't look too closely at the stucco-and-timber walls, one of the rooms looks like any other cidery—lots of large steel and fiberglass tanks filled with bubbling potions. The other room is more unusual. Arrayed along one wall are wooden racks (*pupitres* in French), each studded with scores of bottles standing arse-end up. Imagine sandwich boards perforated with holes the size of a champagne bottle's neck. If my count was

En Français

Many of the techniques used in cider making come from the wine world—and vintners are often touchy about reappropriation. Winemakers from the Champagne region of France invented the technique of disgorgement known as the *méthode champenoise*—a term they claim as their own. The same technique used elsewhere (or, heaven forbid, used to make *cider*) is definitionally *not* the *méthode champenoise*. As a consequence, you may hear the term *méthode traditionnelle*. Making cider in the typical French manner, with natural fermentation and carbonation—but without disgorgement—is sometimes called the *méthode ancestrale*. Subtle differences, but they mean a great deal in France.

accurate, each side of the sandwich board contains 216 bottles—around 3,000 in all.

What are they doing there?

Let's back up a step. One of the by-products of natural fermentation is a light dusting of yeast cells that settle to the bottom of a bottle of cider. After three months, the cider becomes clear and sparkling, but the moment the cork comes off the bottle, all that trapped gas will agitate the yeast, slightly clouding the cider. This cloudiness disturbed the French mind. Going to all the trouble of naturally fermenting, carbonating, and clarifying and then everything gets cloudy? To avoid that minor imperfection, winemakers in the Champagne region came up with an incredibly laborious process known as the *méthode champenoise* (the Champagne method). Few cider-makers go through the bother, but Cyril Zangs is one of them. And what a bother!

Zangs goes through the normal procedure for bottle fermentation, though he caps rather than corks his bottles. (This is another reason he lets the cider go drier than most of his colleagues do—there's no risk of explosion in a capped bottle.) Then he places them on the racks at a forty-five-degree angle. For the next three weeks, he will turn each bottle "nearly a quarter" turn every day. This process is known as "riddling" (or *remuage* in French) and the goal is to slowly work the lees down the bottle and into the neck. It's a tricky business because the particles have different density. "The heavy yeast goes down quick," Zangs explains, "but the light one always stays back. So, if you do it too quick—poof—the big one goes and you will never get the light one back. The big one [pushes] the small one at the same time."

This riddling process is labor-intensive and big companies have automated it. I saw one of these machines in action at Le Face Cachée de la Pomme in Quebec. The bottles are placed in a large crate and trussed up on a mechanical device that slowly moves the entire crate, rather than each bottle. It takes Zangs a half hour to rotate each of his three thousand bottles, but the machine does it in a matter of seconds. As the days go on, Zangs also adjusts the angle of each bottle so that as the yeast nears the neck, the pitch gets steeper.

If Zangs has done his riddling properly, in three weeks' time there will be a small puck of yeast resting on the upside-down bottle cap. Next comes disgorgement (*dégorgement*), when the puck is removed. Normally he sets aside two long, sticky days to work through the whole batch, but on the day I visited, he demonstrated with a single bottle. The contents are under explosive pressure, so the first thing he does is don a rubber jacket—after a couple hours, it will be running with rivulets of cider. The process is pretty much what it sounds like—a pop of the cap and the puck is "disgorged" and sent skyward, along with a spray of mist. There is a trick, however. In order to do it properly, the disgorger holds the bottle neck down while fitting a church key onto the cap. Then he lifts it slowly, allowing the pocket of gas to ascend to the bottle's neck. He must open the bottle at the same moment the gas arrives or it will disturb the yeast and send it in a cloud back into the bottle. If that happens, he has to riddle the bottle all over again.

It's odd that opening the bottle doesn't damage the level and balance of carbonation, but it doesn't. This is one of those benefits to natural carbonation. Zangs disgorges when it's still cold, so the carbon dioxide is already pretty lazy—but the real reason has to do with how well integrated it has become into the cider. After disgorgement, he has to re-cap each bottle, and because he's lost some of the cider during disgorgement, he has to use some of the disgorged bottles to top off the others.

At the end of it all, Zangs will have spent an extra month preparing his cider, hours and hours riddling and disgorging, and he will even end up with fewer bottles than he started with—all in the service of avoiding a little cloudiness. No, his ciders may not be typical for the region, but my, they are still *très française*.

Calvados and Pommeau

Calvados is not well-known in the United States. To Americans, *brandy* means "grape" and Cognac and possibly Armagnac spring to mind. When I've described Calvados to Americans, they seem to anticipate something unserious and medieval—"apple brandy" sounds like something Bilbo Baggins would drink. In fact, Calvados is one of the world's most complex liquors. I am by no means a brandy expert, and so when I cast around for an analogue, my mind fixes on whisky. There's an enormous range between Lowland malts, light and refreshing as spring water, and smoky, aggressive Islay malts. In this way, too, I have found a range in Calvados that takes it from a sweeter, fruit-forward spirit to one that, like Islay whisky, is dry, complex, and assertive. Like whisky, Calvados is a product of the alchemy wrought by terroir, wood, and age.

Christian Drouin's Calvados is made back at the picturesque farmhouse in Coudray-Rabut. The family has dubbed it Coeur de Lion ("lion heart"), a fitting name for such a grand place. The historic *pressoir* is where the cider is distilled, and the Drouins have turned it into a working museum that includes the old apple press the family once used. The old mobile still, made in 1946, stands out in front like an ornament, but it is actually still in use. By law, Pays d'Auge Calvados must be distilled twice, like Cognac, and in fact the main still, housed inside the *pressoir,* was originally built to produce Cognac.

Calvados begins with cider, but not the same cider that goes into bottles, with tons of residual sugar. For distillation, it is fermented completely dry. As the cider distills, the first portion to emerge is known as the "head," and it is aromatic and aggressive. That portion is put aside. The heart comes next—it's the portion that will go on to be distilled a second time. Prior to redistillation, it's known as the *petite eau.* The tail comes last, and it contains vegetal, fatty flavors. The head and tail will go back in with cider and be distilled in a subsequent batch and become *petite eau.* After the first distillation, the heart will only be around 30 percent alcohol by volume. The process repeats with the heart, but the resultant spirit will now be 70 percent alcohol.

At this point, the young brandy (*eau de vie de pomme*) is ready for aging, where it will transform from a clear, rough liquor to a rich, amber one. A lot of chemistry happens in the casks, and it continues the whole time the Calvados ages, whether that's the minimum three years or three decades.

Aging takes a *lot* of space. As we moved around from building to building, we found barrels stacked floor to ceiling, tucked into nooks, and crowding passageways. To get a twenty-year-old stock—far from ancient among Calvados-makers—Drouin needs to stash several barrels for each year. After two decades, he will have stowed dozens of casks and have yet to put a drop in a bottle. (In fact, this is exactly what the founder, Christian Drouin, did.)

Clearly, the age is a critical element for Calvados. Guillaume explained the process. "There are three things that happen together. The first thing is the contact with the wood. The wood gives color at first, but it will mainly give tannins—that's part of the structure of the Calvados—and new flavors. The second thing is oxidation. The Calvados is always in contact with the air, and this completely transforms the flavors." Oak is porous; not enough to let the liquid out, but enough to let oxygen in. "The young spirit smells like fresh apple. With time in the cask, the flavors will move to baked apples, ripe apples, apple marmalade, and, at the end, dry fruits. That's due to the oxidation." When people talk about the age of a liquor, they always mean the amount of time it was aged on wood, not once it was bottled. Because of the oxidation, the cask creates a dynamic environment. Each barrel will contribute slightly different qualities to the liquor. This is why, when distillers release vintages of Calvados, they all have their own character. Once any spirit is put into a bottle, it quits changing and, as a result, quits aging.

Guillaume continued, "And the last thing is evaporation; 3.8 percent is our annual loss. Evaporation is very important because of what it brings—first of all, it will concentrate the Calvados, so an old Calvados will stay in your mouth very long, it will get very rich, and at the same time what evaporates first is the aggressivity. Everything that is hard, aggressive evaporates at first." In the cask, the evaporation reverses the process of the still; it is the liquor that departs, and water stays behind. Because the Calvados begins life as a 70 percent spirit, this actually works to the distiller's benefit. In order to bottle young Calvados, distillers must slowly add water in to bring it back down to the standard 40 percent, but old Calvados descends on its own.

How to Taste Calvados

When Guillaume Drouin poured out the first sample of his Calvados, a 1991, I seized the glass and started swirling it vigorously to release the aromas. He was polite enough to address this faux pas obliquely, by ignoring it and telling me a story about haughty Parisian sommeliers. "If you give Calvados to an experienced sommelier, usually what he does is very offensive for us. He does this." Guillaume then put his own glass flat on the table and swirled it hard, like I had a few minutes earlier. "That's good for wine," he said, "but with Calvados, what you get if you do that is the perception of alcohol." Instead, you want to be very gentle with Calvados. Hold the glass at an angle and slowly turn it, coating the inside. "Wait a little bit until all the aggressive flavors go out. When you see that he is halfway [down the inside of the glass], you bring that slowly to your mouth to get all the complexity at once. That's the trick."

As we walked from room to room, I could see all the variables at play. In one, the casks were all standard wine barrel–size, but in another, each was a slightly different shape. (An old Calvados-maker's trick to fool the tax man.) We came into a room and Guillaume stopped and sampled the air. "This is a good room," he said. "The temperature is always the same, there's good humidity in here. This room makes very mellow Calvados." This reminded me of one of my favorite whiskies, Scapa, from the Orkney Islands. It is aged in warehouses on the sea, and after sixteen years it actually imparts a subtle briny scent. I wanted to ask if this was an element of a Calvados's terroir, but Guillaume had already gone ahead.

If Calvados turns out to be one of the most sophisticated spirits, the odd beverage known as Pommeau does warrant a reputation as rustic and old-timey. Bilbo Baggins may well have had a bottle in his cupboard. The historical record fails to include Pommeau's invention, but it seems a pretty safe bet that farmers have been making it for a long time. Pouring enough Calvados into unfermented juice to raise it to 15 percent will kill off the yeast and bacteria, sterilizing the juice and making it fit for storage—science that cider-making farmers would have understood for centuries.

Pommeau's range may not be quite as broad as Calvados's, but individual products have their own character. Some are heavy and sweet as treacle, while others are more nuanced, with a fruitiness backed up by structure. They have the quality of dessert wine and, like them, have a small target where the richness and complexity come together. Drouin's Pommeau is built to mitigate sweetness and display the tannins of the fruit and character of the Calvados. As Guillaume explained, "The way I understand Pommeau is that it shouldn't be too sweet. I don't want it to be too heavy."

Drouin does this by making a special juice of apples that have lots of bitterness and not so much sugar. Pressed fresh, the juice still tastes sweet, but it has other flavors that will harmonize with the Calvados. Putting the blend on wood helps draw out complexity. By law, once the juice and Calvados are blended—with Calvados composing 25 to 33 percent of the mixture—they must age in a barrel at least fourteen months. Christian Drouin Pommeau spends three years in the barrel and is made with a blend of Calvados vintages from four to ten years old. "We age it longer to give more time to the Pommeau to get rounder, smoother, and well-integrated," said Guillaume. "It's an easy taste." As we drank it, he gave some tasting notes. "There's a bit of bitterness, oxidation. Cinnamon, dry fruit." I would add a woody stiffness and a hint of forest floor.

Spending an afternoon with Cyril Zangs is a curious experience—but it seemed to capture something of the essence of the French part of French cider making. Zangs is the most precise cider-maker I ever encountered. He has exacting standards about everything from the condition and cleanliness of his fruit to the painstaking process of preparing his bottles for disgorgement. After touring his cidery, we had returned to his home and were finishing up our meeting at his rustic dining room table with a sampling of his ciders. I asked how he knew he had made a good cider. "It's very simple. When you drink it, it has to make you [feel] good." He regarded the cider. "It is just evident."

I wouldn't have known how to interpret that had it been the first thing he told me, but after listening to him talk about cider, I think I understood what he meant. The French go through the most steps between harvest and bottling to arrive at their cider, but the idea is to achieve a kind of perfect simplicity. If he does his part right, the cider should express itself in its own natural way. "Everything is in the fruit," he told me. Some years he has more bitter fruit, some years more sweet. He doesn't make his cider to fit a profile; his techniques allow the cider to reveal itself. "I just take my varieties and I make my ciders the best I can with what I get."

Guillaume Drouin, who makes entirely different kinds of ciders, told me almost the same thing. "My philosophy is to do as little as possible with the cider. I don't like this idea of cooking, you know?" (By "cooking," he was referring to the vintner's approach of con-structing a wine.) "The less I can do, the happier I am." It's like a Zen koan. The essence of French cider could be summarized as "from complexity, simplicity."

SAGARDOTECA
70 KM

5 BREAKING THE CIDER

It wasn't that long ago that I learned Spain was famous for its ciders, and this struck me as unbelievable. How could such a hot, dry place be known for the same drink as sodden Somerset? The answer lies in a band of green running from the edge of France across Spain's northern sea coast—in fact, it's called *España Verde* (Green Spain). It contains two of the country's wettest regions, Asturias and the Basque Country, and these happen to be precisely where the apple trees thrive.

On the day I arrived, the skies over Bilbao were liquid. Darting out from underneath the broad cantilevered airport roof was like entering a waterfall. An hour east, Donostia–San Sebastián, in the heart of the cider country, gets about 173 centimeters [68 inches] of rain a year. (New Orleans gets 64 inches.) Basques live at the tail end of the Pyrenees, an area where the lower hills have been an open invitation to conquerors passing between France and Spain. But, while the elevations may be lower here than farther up the spine of the Pyrenees, the Basque hills are nevertheless so steep that the trip along the ribbon of asphalt between Bilbao and Donostia produces a sense of vertigo. Along the way, clouds accentuate the effect, clinging to the sides of the spiky peaks, bathing them in water that keeps them emerald green year-round.

Another feature of the Basque lands that intrigues a visitor is the way the towns are placed at the bottom of valleys. Even in small villages, Basques build sizeable buildings, so as you wheel around a wide turn up on the saddle between two rises, you often look out at the tops of buildings that descend to the valley floor below, making the towns themselves appear tall and vertical. I had an especially good sense of this as I got lost in the heights above Gernika. I was looking for the famous oak tree under which Basques have gathered to decide their fate for centuries. But as I climbed, following one smaller lane after another, I eventually ended up in front of a farmhouse with nowhere else to go. On the way back into town, I could see the whole valley filled up with those strange, high structures, making the little town of sixteen thousand feel like an urban metropolis. Abandoning maps, I decided to drive by instinct. I figured the most famous landmark in the country couldn't be that hard to find.

Most people in the province of Gipuzkoa speak Basque, and of course most people also speak Spanish. The Basque Country straddles Spain and France, and Gipuzkoa, the province where most of the cider is made, borders France; if a Gipuzkoan speaks a third language, therefore, it's often French. Finding someone who speaks English is no simple task. For my visit to the Isastegi cidery in Tolosa, Aitor Izaguirre arranged to have his wife, Ainhoa, come in after work and provide the service. As we were making introductions, she was spelling out names for me, and I acknowledged her relationship, thinking she shared a name with Aitor. "Ah, no; we don't do that here. I keep my surname. He is Aitor Izaguirre and although we are married, my surname is Lobedegi." I was being introduced to one of the many fascinating idiosyncrasies of Basque culture. Casual visitors don't see them, but they stud the Basque Lands like invisible monuments—markers of a culture older than most in the world.

A wife keeping her surname wasn't especially odd. But then she started explaining how names work, and that's when we got to the curious part. "My first surname is my father's first," she began. "My second name is my mother's first. My third is my father's second, which is my father's mother's [maiden name]. I can go, go, go. My mother's first one, which is my second, is my mother's father's first one. At the same time, my mother's father's father's first one. I know eight—easy." Just with their names alone, Basques outline their personal history and their relationships to community, all but invisible to those of us who look confusedly on.

The Basques appeared to the Romans, who found them in 218 B.C., to already be an old people. They are so self-contained that they have their own language, unrelated to any other, their own sports, their own breeds of farm animals, their own laws and taxes, and their own food. (They even have their own font, a typeface that resembles rough-hewn lumber and is visible on any storefront—or bottle of cider.) The one thing they lack is a country. Basques have the misfortune to reside in the easiest access point in the Pyrenees, a place passable even in winter, and for millennia invaders have swept back and forth through *Euskal Herria*—Basque Country. As far back as the Roman period, the Basques had to contend with outsiders, and they decided early how to handle this. Essentially, "If you must claim *Euskal Herria* to please your king, do so, but leave us alone." They kept their ways, ignoring the invaders who planted flags and spoke foreign tongues. After the Romans came the Visigoths, then Muslims from North Africa. The Franks, Normans, and Vikings all fought the Basques as well. Finally, of course, it was the Spanish king who claimed *Euskal Herria* for himself.

Through all these invasions, the Basques developed ways to preserve their culture. One of the most important was a collection of ancient laws called the Fueros that existed for centuries even before they were written down in the eleventh century. Even as foreign kingdoms claimed *Euskal Herria*, by ancient tradition the Basques continued to meet to uphold their commitment to the Fueros, and they did it under an oak tree in the town of Gernika. The town is the seat of the Basque semiautonomous government, and the first stop I made. If Basques have a spiritual capital, it is here.

Gernika

The legislative building in Gernika is modest by comparison to some of the world's grand halls, and the current *Gernikako Arbola* (their meeting oak), planted in 1986 and a descendant of earlier trees, is itself not a soaring giant. But for those who have learned the long history of the Basque people, including the horrors that happened in that city, it seems suitably hallowed.

The first decades of the twentieth century marked a flowering for Basque nationalism in the *Euskal Herria*. In the early months of the Spanish Civil War in the 1930s, the Basques, siding with the legal government, won brief autonomy. It was not to last. The leader of the insurgents, Francisco Franco, after a failed assault on Madrid, set his eyes on the industrial port of Bilbao. Franco appealed to the Nazis and Italians for support, and the fascist war machine began an assault on the Basques by bombing civilians in April 1937. Hundreds were killed, but it was nothing compared to what happened on April 26. Choosing a market day when the streets of Gernika were swollen with villagers from the town and neighboring countyside, the planes spent three hours methodically dropping 90,000 kilograms [99 tons] of explosives and reducing the town to dust. It was one of the first raids on civilians that would come to mark WWII.

International outrage followed the incident, heightened by *Guernica*, a mural Pablo Picasso painted for the 1937 Paris World's Fair (Picasso used the Spanish, rather than Basque, spelling). But it did nothing to help the Basques, who saw their very brief moment of self-rule end in August of that year. Decades later, after their tormentor Franco was planted in the ground, the Basques won some autonomy, which they oversee from the government buildings in Gernika.

There is a strange twist to the story of Gernika that serves as a fitting Basque coda to the events of 1937: The ancient oak, such an important symbol of Basque self-rule, was not damaged in the raid. It was on the edge of town, but apparently the Germans didn't realize what it meant to the Basques. So many conquerors have come to the Basque Country over the millennia, and like so many before, they didn't understand the people they were trying to conquer. The fascists have all faded away, but the *Gernikako Arbola* is now in the center of the rebuilt Gernika in an honored location.

It's difficult to overstate the importance of the Fueros, both as a symbol but also a statement of being. The Fueros are the document that makes those invisible monuments visible. Writer Mark Kurlansky wrote a wonderful history of the Basques, and he describes them this way, "They comprised both commercial and criminal law, addressing a wide range of subjects, including the purity of cider, the exploitation of minerals, the laws of inheritance, the administration of the farmland, crimes and punishments, and a notably more progressive view of human rights than was recognized in Castilian law."

Including the purity of cider. Here is where Basque history intersects with our own; like so many other visible and invisible artifacts, cider is an ancient fixture in Basque culture.

As early as the eleventh century, cider played such a key role in Basque life that they felt it warranted protection in the Fueros. This legacy lives on in Gipuzkoa, which is blanketed by apple trees. People have always made cider here. Although there are many local commercial cideries now, farmers still make their own cider. I asked makers where they learned how to make cider and got confused looks. At Sarasola they told me, "Everybody makes cider." At Isastegi, Ainhoa Lobedegi told me, "Every farm had its own press, so they knew how to make it. Wine was something for Christmas maybe. My father makes cider. They make maybe two thousand liters for home. His friends, too."

In one of the more lurid anecdotes, Kurlansky describes the case of a French judge and witch-hunter in the 1600s who helped carry out the Inquisition. He was incredibly suspicious of the Basques, whose ways he didn't understand, and which all seemed to point to infiltration by the devil. "This is apple country; the women eat nothing but apples, they drink nothing but apple juice, and that is what leads them to so often offer a bite of the forbidden apple." Well, at least he didn't mention the dangers of the terrible fermented juice of the apple.

Celebration of Cider: *Txotx* Season

Here's one thing you need to know about Spanish cider: It is meant to be consumed with food. Eating is a big deal all across the Iberian Peninsula—it may be the thing that most unites Basques with their countrymen. In the course of a day, you'll find people eating at breakfast, during the mid-morning, again at lunch, then stopping off for *pintxos* (Basque tapas) before late dinner. The two largest meals are lunch and dinner and, in the Basque Country, it is typical to have either cider or Basque wine. In the restaurants I visited, diners split about 50/50, with perhaps the slight edge to cider. Unlike the niche place cider has in France and England, in northern Spain it is front and center.

Why does the cider go so well with local food? It doesn't, universally. I learned that the more delicate fillets of hake couldn't stand up to the briny and tart ciders. For those, perhaps a glass of the local white wine, Txakolina, is a better choice. But much of Basque cuisine relies on saltier fish or heavy, bloody steak—flavors that require a bold partner. On their own, Basque ciders can seem one-dimensional in their acidity. These foods draw out their underlying sweetness, though, and make the subtle apple flavors explode; they offer a service to the food as well, cutting through the intense, heavy dishes, refreshing the palate as they go. Once you develop a taste for the funk and acid of Basque ciders, it's a pleasure to drink them alone. Even the biggest fans have to admit, however, that they are at their best on the dinner table.

Tart Spanish Ciders

As cheese lovers must eventually contend with Camembert and Stilton, so the cider fan must come to terms with the world's most unusual expressions—those made in Asturias and the Basque Country of northern Spain. These ciders are made tart, both because of the use of acidic apples and the production of acetic acid during fermentation. Analogous to the place lambics occupy in the beer world, Spanish *sidras*—and especially the Basque *sagardoas*—are the furthest, sour frontier. Their purpose in life is revealed at the dinner table, where the local cuisine, meaty and salty, needs a vivid partner. Spanish ciders aren't for everyone, but for those who love them, all other ciders seem tame and feeble by comparison.

Which brings us to the most enthusiastic celebration of cider in the world—the annual *txotx* season. *Txotx* begins in late January, when the year's first cider has matured and can be served fresh from the giant chestnut-wood casks, and lasts until April, when the warm temperatures force the cider-makers to bottle up their remaining stocks. (In Basque, the "tx" combination is pronounced "ch," so *txotx* sounds like "choach.")

The word comes from the little wooden peg that used to act as a valve in the mammoth Spanish tuns, called *kupelas*; people sampled the cider by removing the peg, sending a slender arc down to waiting glasses. Until about fifty years ago, the celebration of fresh cider was more informal, something done on every farm, but as industry came into the area, commercial cider-makers became more common. In the 1960s, when *txotx* was becoming formalized, locals brought their own bread and stood around the cellar sampling different casks. Eventually, cideries began cooking food themselves, and now hundreds of thousands of people flow into the Basque cider houses to drink up fresh cider and feast on a traditional menu of Basque farmhouse fare. Even though January is not the most pleasant month to do a tour of European cider country, I timed my visit specifically to arrive at the start of *txotx*—it just sounded like too much fun to miss.

Because the towns are compact, Basque Country feels largely rural. It takes only moments to leave the contained little villages, and then you're zipping around twisting roads and shooting up steep hills. In Gipuzkoa, it doesn't take very long before you're passing through orchards, and signs for *sagardotegi* (cider houses) are everywhere. I set out to find Sarasola my first day in Spain. It's a maker of one of the funkiest ciders in the world, and one I developed a taste for in the United States. When I approached the building I took to be Sarasola's, a woman at the *sagardotegi* (cider house) gave me a sour face. I was at the wrong one; Sarasola was *next door*. This is a problem—if you can call it that—with around seventy cideries in an area half the size of Rhode Island. They're lined up literally next to one another.

Recollections differ, but at the Cider Museum in Astigarraga, they reckoned that the standardized menu got fixed sometime around the end of the 1960s. The museum's Ainize Mitxelena explained, "People wanted to drink a good cider, so they came to this village to taste the drinks at the farms. And people, when they went to the different farms, they went with their [own] food. And then, when these new cider houses are open, they begin to give this menu. Why? Because at every farm they have the meat, the fish—the cod—the cheese." Everything on the menu is traditional farm fare, and it seemed the customers started to expect the whole experience.

Now when you walk into a *sagardotegi* during *txotx* season, you know exactly what the menu will be. Or you do after your first visit, anyway; as I strolled into Sarasola, I wasn't sure what to expect. In the informal manner of the Basques, the front door there feels more like the back door—it opens into the cellar, set into the hillside, with a long row of *kupelas* (casks) seemingly leading only deeper into the cellar. However, if you push on, soon scents draw you toward the kitchen—and at mealtimes, that means a grill crackling with the main course—and just past that is a cozy dining room with large, chunky wooden tables.

A man poked his head out of the kitchen and spoke rapid-fire Basque (or *Euskara*, as the Basques call it), and I replied in slow English while pantomiming myself typing. We had engaged in dodgily translated e-mail communication beforehand, and he seemed to expect me. He grinned and gestured to the door, following me through and depositing a plate of blood sausage and chorizo and a bottle of cider on the table. This was, it turned out, a bonus treat. The real first course, a codfish omelet, arrived a quarter hour later, and with it came Javier Quintero, a Colombian who spoke English and acted as my guide for the tour.

Later, when I *txotx*ed at Isastegi, they served food the old way with no plates. Out came a giant omelet and a rustic loaf of bread, and we used forks to pile the former onto thick slices of the latter. At Sarasola, the omelet was sized for two people and came with plates. The Basques have an ancient connection to cod, which is not actually native to their waters. Cod came in the holds of Viking boats in the ninth century. The Basques were perhaps the most accomplished sailors and shipbuilders in the world, and had been providing Europe with whale meat for two centuries before the Vikings came. The Vikings dried cod, which was light and didn't spoil, and the Basques adapted their own technique of whale preservation to make salt cod. Prepared this way, it could be rehydrated into something similar to fresh cod, and they have been eating it ever since. All that history was present in the omelet placed before me—another of the invisible monuments.

I had one mouthful, but then Javier declared it was time for *txotx*. In its current context, the word is strongly connected to the act of drinking from the cask. When you're at the *sagardotegi*, periodic calls ring out: "*Txotx!*" People drop their food and rush to a *kupela*. After the call has been made, a kind of dance begins. One after another, they will collect a splash of cider from a stream that comes straight from the barrel. The way it works is this. The cider-maker or someone from the cidery positions himself at the valve of one of the chestnut tuns. The *kupelas* vary in size, but most are so large that, even resting on their sides, they're taller than a person. To try to keep the spillage to a minimum, cideries place a bucket a little less than two meters [about six feet] in front of the *kupela* where the stream of cider will land—but if drinkers do their part, it will stay dry.

The first person crouches with his glass just over the bucket, where the cider will deliver its greatest impact. Drinkers hold the glass so the stream hits the side, not the bottom, for maximum agitation and aeration. The cider-maker opens the valve, and as soon as the cider starts splashing in his glass, the first drinker lifts it, following the stream upward toward its source. While he's doing that, the next person in the line positions her glass to catch the stream when the first one exits. One after another, people jump in line, and the dance begins. In the course of a busy evening, the summon will come scores of times. This is why the museum's Mitxelena says, "Now 'txotx' is an invitation. We say 'txotx!' Come!"

A long time after the Vikings, during the first Carlist war in 1836, the Basques developed a recipe for preparing salt cod that came from privation. During a siege on Bilbao that year, the people had to live on their salted stores. They learned to make a sauce called *pil-pil* by slowly moving the cod in a pan over low heat, thickening the oil into a creamy sauce. (The name is meant to evoke the sound of sizzling oil.) That was the second dish I received at Sarasola, a variation on the traditional menu, which is often a different preparation of cod.

The next course is the main event, a thick steak. At Sarasola, the meat comes glistening with flecks of rock salt, so not only is it rich and meaty, but salty, too. At Isastegi, the steak is served rare, so bloody, in fact, that Aitor and Ainhoa asked whether I would like them to leave it on the fire a little longer. By that time, it was too late—I had acquainted myself with the Basque way. Bring on the bloody steak and give me a little more *txotx*! The whole thing is a staggering amount of food. By the time the last course came out, I was gasping for air. For dessert, it's whole walnuts, a tangy dry cheese, and quince paste. Even stuffed like a Christmas goose, I still managed to find space to tuck in a few nuts and some of that cheese.

Spanish Cider

These are good examples of the range of Spanish ciders available in the United States.

BEREZIARTUA is one of the more approachable Basque ciders, herbal and not too tart, with a touch of rind-like tannin.

CASTAÑÓN, an Asturian cider, is bristling with surprising spines of tannin, but is balanced with sharp, green-apple acidity.

ESPAÑAR, another Asturian, is a nice entry point for Spanish ciders; it is tart but vinous.

ISASTEGI is a refined Basque cider, with clean, vinous acid and bright apple flavors; when "broken," it turns silky and produces rose and sage.

SARASOLA is the Laphroaig of ciders—you can go no further. It is equal measures acetic and funky, with an earthy base, tart apple, and spice layers.

TRABANCO is the largest brand in Asturias, but don't let that scare you—it has vinegar in the nose, and a palate that suggests pickle, brine, dried herbs, and salt all at once.

Breaking the Cider

One of the curious features of the traditional *txotx* meal is that you don't get a glass of cider and take it back to the table with you. The reason has to do with the momentary state cider assumes after it has been poured from a great height. In both Asturias and the Basque Country, cider is served in a glass the size of an old-fashioned cocktail glass, but one so thin and delicate it's like holding an eggshell in your hand. After the cider splashes into the glass, it is hazy and slightly opaque, clouded by millions of tiny bubbles.

"There is no other way to drink the cider," says Miguel Mari at Isastegi. It must be served this way "to explode it." You never get more than a finger, finger and a half, and according to everyone I spoke to, you must drink it immediately. "You drink what you want in one drink, and then you throw the rest," Mari said, demonstrating by taking a healthy chug of his freshly broken cider and dumping a few remaining drops down a floor drain in Isastegi's cellar room. At the time, I found the whole arrangement incongruous. Isastegi's cellar has a line of the *kupelas* along one wall, big as Volkswagen vans and seemingly built to survive a hurricane. Yet here we were with our impossibly delicate glasses, pouring out only a mouthful to savor before we dumped the rest and returned empty-handed to our meal.

The agitation does a couple things. "The purpose of breaking," Mari explained, "is to release the gases. To bring the scents." What we perceive as flavor is largely aroma, not taste, and agitating the cider seems to break it open. It also enlivens the cider, giving it a sense of momentary carbonation. It both tastes and feels more lively on the tongue. Those tiny bubbles give the cider a silkier, mousse-like texture, and as soon as they escape, it becomes thinner, like water.

All of this is true, and I ran my own, vaguely blasphemous experiment to verify it. Unlike the Basques who live just down the road from these cideries, I was not going to get back to a *txotx* for some time. I wanted to enjoy my cider *with* my meal, so I took the glass back with me. (My hosts at Isastegi actually smiled encouragingly, so it's apparently not too irreverent.) As the cider settles, it does seem to sharpen and flatten out. The acidity asserts itself and some of the floral and appley aromatics faded. But it's also true that even in its slightly less-than-ideal state, it makes a spectacular partner for the food. I was happy to keep up my practice of collecting two fingers of cider and taking some back with me to the table to enjoy with the food. No one seemed to mind.

Throwing the Cider

Unfortunately, one does not always have a *kupela* handy. Sometimes you'll be forced to drink your Asturian or Basque cider from a bottle. If you find yourself in such a situation, take heart—it's still possible to properly aerate your *sidra*. The Asturians charmingly call this "throwing the cider," and it's a wonderfully evocative description.

The technique is easy to describe, but a challenge to master. You begin by holding the bottle high over your head in one hand. With your other hand, you hold the appropriate glass underneath, positioned, as when receiving it from a *kupela*, so that the stream hits the side. In the Basque Country they fit the bottles with little devices that send the cider out at a right angle, but in Asturias they go straight from the bottle. Either way, you pour the cider slowly to create maximum breakage (of the cider, not the glass). The agitated state will last perhaps a minute, losing effervescence by the second, so just pour out a splash and toss it back quickly.

The trick is hitting the target without being able to take in the whole operation at a glance. It takes practice, but I promise you the rewards are immediate. And, once you have it down, it makes quite a party trick.

Basque Cider Making

The city of Donostia crowds around a crescent bay, and the beach it cradles is one of the most famous in Spain. It's an international city mostly known by its Castilian name, San Sebastián, but Gipuzkoans use the Basque. Indeed, on the small lanes that feed into the city, street signs with the official name "Donostia–San Sebastián" often have the latter designation blacked out by spray paint. This emphasizes, lest anyone mistake the coastal jewel's provenance, that Donostia is a Basque town. In addition to the beach are

Donostia's famous restaurants—more decorated than in any city save Paris—bars serving *pintxos*, spectacular old cathedrals, and winding, cobblestone lanes. It's also a great place to drink cider.

One blustery afternoon, I ducked into one of the little restaurants in Donostia's old town for lunch. It is typical that restaurants serve only one brand of cider, and this was a Saizar house. Saizar was unknown to me, so I passed along my appreciation to the waiter. Was it a favorite of his, I asked? "No! We don't think like that," he told me. "We think of the ciders like they are our family. They are a natural product and every one is different." We continued to chat about natural ciders—after visits to England, France, and now two Basque cideries, I was a convert. He spoke dismissively about national brands and fussy cider making. Only natural cider could really be considered real cider. "Once you start putting something in it, it's not cider anymore—it's like wine." In all the cideries in the area, "natural" is the only way to make cider, and the waiter's sentiments are broadly shared.

Basque cider is very much in line with the traditions of England and France. As in those countries, the apples are harvested in three periods during the fall, pressed, and the juice is put away to naturally ferment. The process is nearly identical to the English method. In late September, the low temperatures are still relatively cool, with highs around 21°C [70°F] (5°C warmer than Herefordshire, and 2°C warmer than Normandy). Larger cideries like Isastegi chill their juice to 10°C [50°F], and smaller ones like Sarasola use cellars to keep ambient temperatures in the same range. Fermentation takes four months, and the cider is allowed to go fully dry and still. Basque cider is not carbonated.

Yet still there are some differences. The character of Spanish cider is defined by its vivid acidity—this is true of Asturian cider as well as Basque. Apples are a big part of the explanation. Whereas sharps just inflect the ciders of France and England, in Spain they are the main show, making up at least 50 percent of the blend. The apples are unique to Spain, and in Gipuzkoa, the names are a mouthful: Mozoloa, Geza Gorri, Txalaka, Pelestrina, Urtebi Txiki, Sagar Beltza. There are hundreds of varieties in Asturias and the Basque Country. At the cider museum in Astigarraga, they sell unfermented juice, and you really get a sense of regional particularity. It's unlike any apple juice I've ever tasted—tropical, with spiky acidity and notes of coconut and passion fruit.

The trees are also curious—tiny creatures that grow like shrubs at angles perpendicular to the rolling hills. This is by design, and even on the flatter areas they grow no more than two and a half meters [eight feet or so]. The reason has to do with the difficulty of harvesting on steep hillsides. Machines can't scale the grassy slopes, so the harvest is all done by hand. The farmers shake the trees and then use tools called *kizkia* to gather the apples. This traditional implement consists of a wooden dowel with a steel spike coming off the end at a right angle; harvesters impale the apple and then whack the stick on the side of a basket to send it tumbling onto a growing pile. During harvest season, the sound of tapping fills the air.

Although hilly, Gipuzkoa doesn't have a lot of elevation, which Isastegi's Miguel Mari believes is good for fruit. "The maximum you can find apple trees growing is about 300 meters [985 feet] above sea level. Some people say—but they're just saying, they're guessing—that the higher the apple tree is, the finer the flavor of the apple. The lower the apple tree is, the bigger the apple but also it loses concentration, it's more watery." Mari takes no chances; Isastegi is on a perch above the small town of Tolosa.

And what of these enormous *kupelas*—what role do they play? Any time a fermenting beverage is placed inside wood, it becomes a unique ecosystem as the different compounds and organisms interact. It means that each *kupela* will contain a slightly different cider. Throughout an evening during *txotx* season, each one of a cidery's *kupelas* will be tapped, and over time people begin to develop favorites. The vast majority of Isastegi's cider is aged in steel tanks rather than *kupelas*— those are made to produce a consistent product. But after the *txotx* season, when it's time to bottle up the remaining stocks from the wooden tuns, people return and put in their orders. They may buy up to three hundred bottles from their favorite cask.

At Sarasola, Quintero stopped in front of one *kupela* and announced that it was the best. It was set off slightly from the others, and he thought temperature may play a role. "You don't feel it, but the *sidra*, he can feel it, eh? This is always the best of the best," he said, patting it. He pointed out, though, that the dynamic environment inside the *kupelas* meant that the cider changed over the course of the *txotx* season. "Another mysterious thing I have seen is that maybe today you drink the first *barril* [barrel] and you prefer it. Two weeks later you come and try, and you don't prefer this one. Two weeks ago it is good, right now, no. You like a different one. The natural temperature, the different position of the moon—I don't know, but something."

The Riddle of the Sour

There is no secret about what causes the pucker in Spanish cider— acetic acid. By itself, we call the compound vinegar, and most cider-makers consider it a fault. Not only is it *not* a fault in Spanish ciders, but more than anything else, it's what defines them. When I boarded a plane to Europe, I went with the expectation that my many questions about ciders would be answered by the men who make them. But the more I learned about traditional practices, the more this facet of Spanish cider started to look like a riddle: Why do some ciders develop acetic acid while others do not?

Asturian Cider

The Principality of Asturias, east of the Basque Country, is another of those autonomous regions that line apple-growing Green Spain on the northern coast. In the United States, it's easier to find Basque ciders, but Asturias is, by some margin, the capital of Spanish cider making. Asturians drink the most cider in Spain and make the most cider (80 percent of Spain's total), the towns are studded with *sidrerías*, and the industry is big enough to support large producers like Trabanco and El Gaitero. But as in Normandy, Asturian cider has kept its heritage and devotion to *sidra natural*—natural cider.

The Spanish ciders very much form a continuum. Asturian cider was granted a protected designation for *sidra natural* that outlines where the apples must come from and of what varieties the cider may be made. But one taste of *Sidra de Asturias* is enough to confirm its authenticity. Like the Basques, Asturians like bright, tart ciders. They are fruitier and less tart than Basque ciders, full of fresh, green-apple life.

Sidra natural must be made still and dry—this is the cider made for throwing. The Asturians also carved out local designations for two other varieties, though—ciders of a type you won't find in the Basque Country. "New Expression" (*sidra natural de nueva expresión*) is the name given to natural cider that has been cleaned up a bit through filtration. Fans believe that by removing some of the funkiness, the fruit flavors can move closer to center stage; critics charge that funk *is* Asturian. (I prefer the old expression.) Last is naturally sparkling cider. These also tend to be a little more market-friendly, but *sidra's* native zing takes well to effervescence.

I harbored a suspicion that it had to do with temperature. Cold is a great way to retard the growth of bacteria, so perhaps it was the balmy Spanish air that encouraged the little critters. I then discovered that, while Spain is definitely warmer than England, it's not hugely so, and temperatures are only a few degrees warmer than Normandy. And then I further discovered that the cider-makers take care to ferment at about the same temperature, around 10°C [50°F], as French and English cider. No luck on that theory; strike one.

If you recall the chapter on English ciders, there is the mostly lost style of rough, sour "scrumpy." I first considered the question of acetic acid then, and Tom Oliver explained why it is no longer a problem (or benefit, depending on your preferences) of traditional cider making. He fingered the acetic acid bacteria that get harbored in the wooden barrels and flourish because oxygen seeps in through the porous fiber. I was confident this would emerge as the answer—until I started touring Basque cideries. Because, while it's true that chestnut *kupelas* are to be found in every cidery in the Basque Country, so are stainless-steel vats. Bottles of Isastegi, for example, contain cider that never touched a wooden stave. That cider wasn't picking anything up from wood. Strike two.

As my curiosity grew, I started wondering if it might have to do with the apples themselves. Did they contain special bacteria native to Spain? I did a little evening reading and found a theory that involved the *kiskias*. The writer suggested that puncturing the apples introduced acetic acid bacteria that flourished before the juice was even pressed. I've seen no other mention of this possibility, though, and it feels like another swing and a miss. Strike three?

The answer to the riddle still eludes me, but I did find some interesting reading in the technical journals. ("Interesting" may not be the word everyone would use first.) One study in particular was revealing. Researchers took apples from a single orchard and handled them differently to see what would happen. They divided the fruit in half and pressed one with a traditional (wooden) press and the other with a pneumatic (steel) press. They divided these two batches and aged them each in both wooden and steel *kupelas*, coming up with four different batches of cider made with different combinations of wood and steel. When they ran tests on the four batches, they found that each one was different.

There were three important findings: 1) The acetic acid was produced by the conversion of lactic acid bacteria, not by acetic acid bacteria (those are rough characters like acetobacter that cause spoilage); 2) It is the traditional press, which harbors yeast and bacteria from previous pressings, that is the main cause of acetic acid production, not the *kupelas*; and 3) The lactic acid bacteria from the traditional presses boosted malolactic fermentation, so that the ciders that touched only steel had about twice as much malic acid as those pressed traditionally. Perhaps this helps explain why the perception of sour is still strong even in all-steel ciders.

Whatever the answer, the Spanish cider-makers have it figured out, and the result is evident in every bottle. Sometimes you don't have to know, you just have to taste.

I happened to visit *Euskal Herria* during one of the wettest weeks of the year. There was a dusting of snow on the high peaks and the air was sharp from icy winds. I arrived at Isastegi during a rare cloud break, just as the sun was setting—but it was still cold. Basque farmhouses are sturdy structures and often large—and Isastegi is housed in a grand building that glowed warmly from inside. Miguel, Ainhoa, and Aitor all greeted me at the door, and we stepped into the portion of the building that housed the cellars and dining room. Someone had started a fire that crackled merrily in a large stone fireplace, and we gathered around with our hands out toward the heat.

Later on, after the tour, more family members trickled in to join us for our *txotx* meal. As we were literally breaking bread (well, cutting—Aitor was manning the knife), Ainhoa tried to explain the place of cider in their lives. It was not an exalted one, but it was ubiquitous. "The Basque Country has always been rural; we have farms on our lands," she told me. "We had our animals, our cows, our pigs, our hens; they ate and drank what they produced at home. Cider is part of that. The Basque people—any celebration is around a table. Big families. A farm needed a lot of people to work. So you need a lot of food, a lot of drink."

Throughout the night, the call for *txotx* rang out regularly. Aitor's father took a special interest in my cider education, and even though neither of us spoke a word of the other's language, he used his hands and facial expressions to provide good instruction about how to catch, drink, and enjoy Miguel's handiwork. A *txotx* meal lasts a long time, and we weren't in any hurry. The Basques have a hidden culture, but it's not secret. Next to that fire, with my belly full and my favorite *kupela* identified (number twelve), I had a fleeting experience of being a Basque. It's a rare treat to find an access point into culture, but cider does that for anyone who visits Gipuzkoa in the *txotx* season. In front of those giant *kupelas*, we're all Basque, at least for a couple hours.

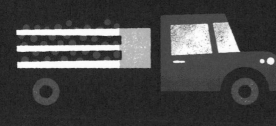

6

THE
AMERICAN
CIDER
RENAISSANCE

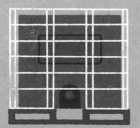
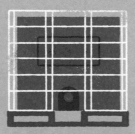

The rolling countryside of western New England looks like apple country. In the fall, when the leaves turn to fire, you expect to see a clapboard farmhouse surrounded by gnarled trees, like something out of a story by Nathaniel Hawthorne ("where the big piles of golden and rosy apples lie under the orchard trees, in the mild, autumnal sunshine"). Outside of Lebanon, New Hampshire, there is just such a place, and its antiquity isn't faked. The white farmhouse dates to the eighteenth century and looms on a small rise, and as you pull into the lane, an orchard that looks like it might date back to Hawthorne's time seems ready to swallow you up. This is Poverty Lane Orchards and Farnum Hill Ciders, and its owners, Stephen Wood and Louisa Spencer, have done more to revive traditional American cider than anyone else in the country.

My first visit came on the last day of harvest, near Halloween. Dawn brought a few flakes of snow, but by the time I arrived at the orchard it was a perfectly luminous, crisp fall morning. Steve greeted me in front of the cow barn—which turned out to double as the cidery—and offered me one of his giant hands. Men who work in fields grow hands like shovels, and Steve got his start in the orchards in 1965. Even though he's been making cider for over two decades (three, depending on how you count), he still describes himself as an orchardist, as if cider making were merely a downstream complication.

He was dressed like an orchardist, with a wool sweater as thick as a parka along with a canvas coat that seemed to be in service mainly for the bulging pockets. We went immediately to the barn, an antique structure with ribs still showing the bite of old colonial handsaws. In order to fashion it into a cidery, he'd had to do a minor refit—but it still looks mostly like an old barn. In one corner there's a stout steel tank, and in front of the doors, an array of wine barrels; the very

Orchard Not Necessary

I am an Oregonian and therefore acquainted with the way wineries work. I point my car west, and when the lush land begins to undulate and grow rows of grapevines, I know I'm in wine country. When I began touring cideries, I did roughly the same thing, following GPS instructions, all the while scanning for apple trees. It turns out that's not how most American cideries work.

As Steve Wood explained, forty years ago apples became a commodity. They're produced in bulk and the juice is stored in quantity. Anyone can buy that juice, so all a cidery really needs to get started is a small industrial space with tanks in which to ferment it. Most of what's available on the market comes from eating apples, and the juice isn't particularly interesting—though cider-makers can get some character by blending. There's even a small source (one currently dwarfed by demand) of juice available from orchards with cider trees—for example, in addition to making his own cider, Steve Wood sells juice to cider-makers. As cider continues to grow in popularity, many makers are contracting with growers to provide fruit, including apples from newly planted cider varieties. For many cideries, it makes sense to leave the growing to the experts.

sharp-eyed might notice the floor looked a bit more modern—the kind of level surface critical to moving heavy containers of liquid. It was, of course, unheated, and I immediately began to covet Steve's wool.

If you Google the words "American cider," you're going to find lots of stories about Steve Wood and his Farnum Hill Ciders. The *New*

York Times, Washington Post, National Public Radio, Slate.com—lots of national news organizations have been covering the revival of cider in America, and they all beat a path right to this barn. The country may have a long and storied history with apple cider, but it's a fractured one. There's no taproot to link the modern era back to anything like traditional cider making—that was lost many long decades ago. Cider making only got revived recently, and to the extent there's anything like a developing American "tradition," it began when orchardists like Steve and Louisa first started grafting trials at Poverty Lane in the early 1980s.

The continent's first infatuation with cider came in the early seventeenth century, when cider-drinking English settlers arrived. North America does have native crab apple varieties, but none that were apparently much use to the people already here. If you recall the stories of the hard early years Europeans endured on their new continent, the apple tree looks like one element of salvation. Apples provided nutrition and a source of sugar and could be preserved whole or in liquid form. To English immigrants used to unclean water, cider was thought to be a necessity. The earliest domestic apples were harvested around 1623 in Boston and, within a few decades, new North American varieties were springing up around New England. One of the earliest was the Roxbury Russet, an apple you can find at Poverty Lane (though not much of it—Steve much prefers Golden Russet).

Settlers grew apples as far south as Georgia. They spread in part by graft, but just as often by seed. This in turn led to an explosion of new domestic varieties. Farmers let seedlings get big enough to produce fruit and took grafts from those that bore tasty apples. John Chapman, known to history as Johnny Appleseed, was the most famous evangelist for planting seedling apples, helping push them out into the "west"—Ohio and Indiana. But by the time he was spreading the word (and seeds) in the early 1800s, apples were already an article of religion in America.

In the first years of the new nation, there were three locations particularly noted for cider. New England was the most organized, receiving encouragement from the Massachusetts Agricultural Society to breed and grow cider fruit. They may not have needed much encouragement, though; farmers couldn't grow barley to make beer, so apples were the go-to source for fermentable sugars. At independence, one in ten farms had cider mills and everyone—men, women, and children—drank it. Per capita consumption was thirty-five gallons a year.

Observers of the time also praised Virginia ciders for their quality. It was another of the most important early cider regions, and the place that gave us the Hewe's Crab apple. But the name of the town most associated with apples at the time was in between New England and Virginia. To modern ears, the name just doesn't sound bucolic, but it was: Newark, New Jersey. This was home to the country's best cider, and also its best apple, the Harrison. William Coxe, writing in 1817, called it "the most celebrated of the cider apples of Newark . . . it produces a high-colored, rich, and sweet cider of great strength." Coxe goes on to mention that Essex County was producing six million gallons of cider in 1810—a staggering quantity for a product that did not lend itself to mass production.

By the time John Hancock signed the Declaration of Independence in 1776, cider had been a major part of American culture for 150 years. Many people think it lasted another 150, until Prohibition would deal a fatal blow, but that overstates its stay. People reviewing the history of American cider inevitably come to the Presidential election of 1840 as an illustration of cider's enduring popularity—but that's the moment we can actually see it fade from American life.

In the campaign, William Henry "Tippecanoe" Harrison and John Tyler used images of log cabins and cider barrels as symbols of their authenticity against patrician incumbent Martin Van Buren—the 1840s version of running on Mom and apple pie. But this misses the context of the campaign, which illustrates that contemporaries thought log cabins and cider stood for something very different from authenticity—they signaled obsolescence. Harrison was sixty-seven, and critics mocked him as borderline senile. In fact, it was a Democratic newspaper in Baltimore, mocking Harrison, that gave him the symbols he'd ride to the White House. "Give him a barrel of hard cider, and settle a pension on him," wrote John de Ziska, and "he will sit the remainder of his days in his log cabin by the side of the fire and study moral philosophy!"

The point: Harrison was as obsolete as log cabins and cider. Not Mom and apple pie—gramophones and leisure suits.

By the time that election was over, cider was already becoming a lost art. In his 1822 edition of *The American Orchardist*, James Thacher wrote about cider like it was a vibrant part of American life. But barely more than a generation after Tippecanoe's triumph, J. S. Buell wrote a volume to try to revive interest in what was clearly a lost art. "Most people are familiar with the juice of apple under the name cider, while an exceedingly limited number know anything about the wine which may be obtained from the apple." In fact, the obituary was right there in the campaign materials of 1840, which used the words "hard cider," rather than the common use of "cider" that was common in Thacher's day. By sometime around the halfway mark of the nineteenth century, hard cider had become a footnote in American life.

Why Cider Vanished

In 1990, cider was essentially extinct in the United States and had been since the start of Prohibition in 1920. Prohibition usually gets credit for delivering the *coup de grâce*, but that exaggerates cider's state of health *before* 1919. By 1915, Americans drank just thirteen million gallons of the stuff—less than 1 percent of the beer produced that year. It had been dwindling for decades, and ceased to have a significant national presence since the 1850s. What happened?

Everything from urban migration to the temperance movement gets the blame, but many of the explanations fail to convince. (The rural population barely fell between 1790 and 1860—from 96 to 84 percent—and the temperance movement certainly wasn't driving *whisky* out of business.) I think the reasons are partly cultural and partly technological. Early-American cider was essentially a farmhouse product, beholden to the seasons. It was difficult to streamline the process or make it on an industrial scale. That was fine for the agrarian country at independence, but as the nation began to flex its industrial muscles, cider making couldn't keep up.

The second factor was beer. It was hard to grow good barley or hops in the United States, and for long decades, what was brewed was neither particularly good nor popular. Instead, the United States was a liquor country, and we drank vats of the stuff. That changed in the mid-nineteenth century, when legions of well-trained German brewers started immigrating, bringing their lager-making technology with them. They figured out how to work with rough American barley and hops, and, all of a sudden, Americans developed a taste for beer. In 1810, there were only 140 commercial breweries in the country; fifty years later there were more than 2,500. Production increased twentyfold.

This wave of immigration coincided with an era of technological innovation, turning brewing into an industrial enterprise. Like other industries, brewing specialized. Farmers grew the ingredients, maltsters turned grain to brewing malt, brewers made the beer, and distributors sent it in rail cars around the country. Breweries could make beer twelve months a year and were only limited by the size of their industrial plants. Cider, by contrast, was made on the same farm where the apples were grown. It would be decades before refrigeration and concentration would make it possible to scale up production. Cider got the reputation of a bumpkin's drink—rough, backwoods, old-timey.

Cider was a goner long before people left the farms or started to agitate for abstinence. It's worth noting, though, that those later developments—urban migration, the shift of apple-growing westward, temperance and Prohibition—played a different role. They may not have caused cider's demise, but they certainly doomed its quick revival. After Prohibition ended in 1933, breweries, wineries, and distilleries were still around and went back into business. Cider . . . not so much. It would take a few more decades before anyone thought to revive it; and by then, it was more reinvention than revival.

In the 1970s, just as Steve Wood was taking over the orchards in New Hampshire, the business was getting difficult for family farmers. Apples had become an international commodity. Supermarkets were looking for Technicolor, wax-dipped giants to attract customers' eyes. In an era before "heirloom," smaller, imperfect apples were a hard sell. But even worse, as Wood explained, "we also knew we couldn't possibly compete on the hillsides of northern New England in production efficiency with other players." Even if they did produce supermarket-ready fruit, they couldn't make money growing it.

At the time, cider was remembered by Americans in the same manner as the cotton gin—something important to history, maybe, but for reasons long forgotten. It didn't occur to Steve and Louisa to turn their crops to liquid. Then, on a trip to England in the early 1980s, Steve saw the future. "We were taking a trip from Wales to London though Hereford and passing through *weird* orchards and—poor Louisa—I pulled over to the side of the road to see what the hell I was looking at. I found I was in one of the cider districts of England." It took years for them to begin to see a future as cider-makers, but in that moment they saw that there were other uses to which apples might be put.

Steve and Louisa began looking into cider very gingerly. They made contact with the legendary Bertram Bulmer, who was at the time already into his sixth decade as chairman of HP Bulmer, and went on to consult with other cider-makers and researchers in England and France. It didn't take very long before they were conducting grafting trials of several hundred different varieties of European cider and American heirloom apples. In this early stage, Steve was mainly focused on seeing which varieties would grow—and indeed, which samples of the scion wood were even true to variety. "Tremlett's Bitter and Yarlington Mill," he found, "were two that are all over the country by those names but aren't those apples."

Even years after they had begun to get a handle on which apples grew well in New Hampshire, they were still thinking like apple growers, not cider-makers. Steve was anticipating the market and wondering if they could sell heirloom varieties. "Then it struck us that we had a decade of horticultural experience with a few hundred uncommon varieties on this ground and we'd already figured out that among those varieties there were a handful that we really grow the hell out of here." In 1989, they planted a thousand cider trees and, although they hadn't quite come to terms with it, set their future as cider-makers into motion.

Just a couple years after Steve and Louisa were speeding through the orchards of Herefordshire, Morgan Miller was making his first trip to the English West Country. Morgan's story involves a similar love story, as he became transfixed by the ciders he found there. He worked in taverns rather than orchards, though, and when he returned to the United States, Morgan was more interested in promoting cider than making it. Wine had gone through a renaissance, and beer was in the midst of one; he wanted to spark a revival of cider, too.

He considered starting a cider magazine, but when he looked around, he found almost no American cideries. "I think I discovered seven cideries. I *think*." Depending on which source you consult, America produced somewhere between a quarter and three-quarters of a million gallons of cider in 1990. To put that figure in perspective, it's what a modest craft brewery makes in one year. This is why Steve and Louisa were seriously questioning cider's viability, and why Morgan ultimately scrapped his magazine idea. Instead, a few years later, he would use a newfangled technology called "the Internet" to launch a website that functioned as a clearinghouse for all cider activities in America.

Cider started to flourish. The growth was strong enough to encourage orchardists to consider planting cider fruit. Morgan ticked off the various cideries that were opening and the acres put into cider-fruit production. (Things may have been growing, but they were still small enough that he could keep track of individual orchards.) But then things really exploded, and cider grew at an annual clip of 70 percent for the next five years and passed five million barrels in 1996. Wineries and breweries sensed an opportunity and jumped in. More and more, the small, orchard-based producers were being eclipsed by large industrial manufacturers.

"And then," Morgan said, "there was the crash." Beginning around 1997, craft brewing went through a period known retrospectively as "the shake-out," when many overleveraged breweries and speculators saw their production collapse. Unlike beer, which had enough market share to weather the storm, "cider went poof." Morgan believes there were two challenges cider couldn't overcome. It hadn't had enough time to establish itself, and it had been positioned, as Morgan sheepishly described, "as a 'girl-drink,' which was how it was always advertised." This coincided with an explosion in a dubious category known as "alco-pop"—sweet, fizzy, lightly alcoholic drinks. They came in many forms, like Zima, Mike's Hard Lemonade, Smirnoff Ice, and others, but as a category, ciders blended in with them. Morgan writes the obituary for 1990s cider this way: "You can make malt-based alco-pops much cheaper than cider, so why go there?"

The first attempt to establish cider in the United States fizzled by the turn of the new millennium. Some companies managed to survive, but cider had to wait for a second dawn before Americans would rediscover the simple joys of fermented apple juice. That came about a decade later, when "craft cider" finally came of age.

As little as two or three years ago, most Americans were unaware that cider was becoming a thing. In my hometown of Portland, Oregon, in 2010, a brave gentleman named Jeff Smith opened Bushwhacker's, the first full-time cider bar in the United States in what seemed like an admirable, if quixotic, venture. But within a couple years, Smith's bet started to look smart. Cideries started opening almost as fast as

The Three Schools of American Cider

The United States, now in the thick of its second modern cider revival, does not have a single national cider-making technique—it has three. Traditionalists make natural cider in the manner of the Europeans. They follow the methods and practices established in Herefordshire, Normandy, or Asturias, and their ciders, while not mere imitations, recall those European ciders. Modernists look to the wine world, where the methods are designed to strip away everything but the fruit. Practitioners of this school pitch (add) relatively neutral yeast strains, focus on specific apple varieties, and use careful blending to produce the flavors they prefer. The Experimentalists, forced by circumstance to work with eating apples, use any process or ingredient they can to infuse flavor into their ciders. They fiddle with odd fermentations and add other fruit, spices, and even hops to give their Red Delicious and Gala ciders more zip.

breweries in the Pacific Northwest, and pubs and restaurants started putting them on tap lists. National brands have become successful, sparking brewing giants AB InBev and MillerCoors to belatedly launch their own brands in 2014 (Johnny Appleseed and Smith & Forge).

But unlike the last wave of American cider, this one looks different. Morgan Miller, who by now has been watching the market for nearly thirty years, thinks American cider has finally come of age. "The biggest change I've seen is that it's now seen as a legitimate drink unto itself." The biggest change since the 1990s is that now there is a "craft" cider segment. As with wine and beer before it, Morgan continues, "People are quick to recognize that there are different tiers to cider; there are different flavor profiles."

Having more sophisticated customers means cider-makers can pursue their own fascinations rather than trying to make mainstream ciders to appeal to a mass audience. "It's almost like we all got the same idea about four or five years ago," says Sharon Campbell of Washington's Tieton Cider Works. "And then we're all interpreting that idea in a very different way."

The American cider landscape is still wild and largely unsettled. There are cider-makers who farm their own cider fruit and make products from the European tradition, and there are cider-makers who buy juice by the truckload and trick it out with spices, other fruits, and funky fermentations. And everything in between. But if we look past the dazzling array of products, I have found three different philosophies that seem to guide American cider-makers. All three see their products as examples of the "American" tradition, yet they are different and in some cases contradictory. But this may be the greatest evidence of their provenance. America is an immigrant country, and our instinct to borrow, reinterpret, and invent *is* our national tradition.

The Traditionalists

When I arranged to tour Kevin Zielinski's orchards, he told me to meet him at the family's Farm Market. It is located on the outskirts of Salem, Oregon, in the Willamette Valley—one of the best growing regions in the world. The rich alluvial soil settled on the valley floor after the last ice age and is now caressed by misty winter rain and dry, mild summers. The Willamette Valley supports, among the nation's largest concentrations of hop, hazelnut, and Christmas tree farms, more than 250 wineries producing celebrated pinot noir. Zielinski's grandfather planted EZ Orchards in 1929, but his mother's side of the family came out in a wagon train in 1850. Locals know the Zielinskis for the annual Harvest Fest at the farm and their little produce store, not cider. And yet within the cider community, Zielinski commands enormous respect for his coruscating, complex French-style ciders.

Kevin met me in the parking lot, and then we hopped in his pickup and drove to the orchards. The Zielinskis have been growing apples and pears on the farm for decades, but the fruit was destined for the grocery store, not the bottle. He took me to a field where the old Jonathan trees had been grafted with cider wood that spring—signs of change at EZ. Being able to graft onto mature trees gives Kevin a head start over other Northwest cider-makers, who are starting out with new trees; the grafts will produce apples more quickly, and because the old rootstock is well established, the trees require less fertilizer. (Later, when he's using natural yeast to ferment the juice, that nutrient balance will keep the fermentation slow and sedate.)

Orchardists use tape to protect new grafts, much like we bandage a wound. Kevin pulled out a pocket knife and peeled back the yellow tape to reveal two pieces of wood spliced together. Grafting doesn't *look* like it should work. Underneath the tape, Kevin revealed a section where the old branch—as thick as my wrist—had been lopped off. The new branch was healthy and thick with leaves, but it did nothing to conceal the line where the old limb had been. At this point, Kevin has enough scion wood from his own trees to change a whole field from dessert fruit to cider fruit.

Kevin didn't intend to become a cider-maker. In 2000, a winemaker approached him with the idea of growing cider apples to make French-style cider. The vintner supplied the scion wood for grafting—twelve varieties of French cider apples. But then, before the trees were producing much volume, he took a job at a Washington state winery, leaving Kevin with an acre of obscure, inedible cider apples.

That was in 2003, long before people were clamoring for cider fruit, but he decided to go ahead and let the apples mature. He knew many winemakers from the valley and had for years made his own wine. Why not try making cider? His first vintage came out in 2007, and he's been refining and expanding ever since.

In the decade and a half since that first orchard went in, Kevin has mostly stuck with French varieties, which make up 85 percent of his blend. I have now visited orchards in five countries, but Kevin seems to relate to his trees more intimately than anyone I've met. As we approached each new variety, Kevin would light up and describe the qualities of the fruit and the growing behavior of the tree, as if they had individual personalities, like people. He'd point out the ones that had bushy habits, or the tall, lanky trees. Not every variety took to Oregon's terroir, and from time to time we'd come across a droopy runt failing to thrive. Even then, he'd call it a "curious" variety, as if it were just misbehaving.

"I didn't have a lot of concern about growing these trees. That's what I am—I'm an orchardist. I've grown probably twenty-plus different types of apples in my career, and they all behave differently. So I can work with that." Some were just bound not to grow well so far from Normandy. But others, like Frequin Rouge, Reine des Pommes, Saint Martin, and Marie Ménard, seem to flourish. One of the tastiest apples I sampled was the Frequin Rouge, a bittersweet with tons of spicy tannin.

With each new variety, the pocketknife would appear in his hand and he'd have plucked and cut the apple almost in a single motion. He cut them horizontally, to reveal the seeds arranged in a star shape inside. As we walked from field to field, he tried to pick especially ripe fruit that had begun to liquefy, or "watercore," near the peel. "It's the conversion of the fruit as it ripens." With one exception, he managed to grab a ripe apple every time. I asked how he could tell which apples were at that level of ripeness. "See how it's a little bit translucent?" he asked, holding up a fully ripe and a not-quite-ripe apple for comparison. I studied the skin, and they looked exactly like each other. He grinned and we bit into it.

PRODUCTION

There are very few Americans making natural cider. This is partly because it's a complicated, time-consuming process, but mainly because to Americans it seems unnecessarily dangerous. Other cider-makers I spoke to seemed startled that I'd even suggest it. But that's how Kevin has always done things. "My wine-making interest was in doing spontaneous ferments, either no use of sulfites or very low use of sulfites and post-malolactic fermentation." The taste of ripe produce is in Kevin's blood, and his orientation in making cider is attention to the fruit. He chose the method of production that he thinks interferes as little as possible with the expression of the fruit we were tasting as we walked around his orchard—harvest-fresh, directly off the trees. "If I'm making cider from fruit, let's let the fruit be the factor that has the most influence."

The method of letting cider ferment itself seemed like a natural fit to Kevin. "I went with a very fruit-sensitive, fruit-aware method of fermentation. I know there are other things happening, but I haven't manipulated them. I think this [spontaneous fermentation] is truer to what the fruit itself would do than if I'd purified it with SO_2 and made a yeast inoculation."

The process he uses is identical to the one employed by cider-makers across Normandy. He uses a similar blend of apples to create a high-tannin juice with relatively low acidity and then ferments it naturally at cold temperatures for months over the winter, racking it often to help strip the cider of nutrients. Then he bottle-conditions the finished cider for months longer. Kevin considers his process very much in the French tradition and even refers to it as the *méthode ancestrale*. He has never used sulfites or any additives, but is considering adding a very small amount as he steps up production with young, nutrient-rich trees.

Kevin doesn't eschew modernity. He uses the press and fermentation vessels at a nearby winery to make his cider, and it is a state-of-the art operation. Unlike the cider-makers of Europe who let the climate chill their juice, Kevin has artificial refrigeration. Nevertheless, the basic process, from start to finish, is just like the one I saw at Christian Drouin in Coudray-Rabut (even the equipment was very similar). This all-natural approach, tree to bottle, is still vanishingly rare in the United States. A few cideries are beginning to put toes very tentatively in the waters of natural fermentation. Former Goose Island brewmaster Greg Hall recently launched Michigan-based Virtue Cider with a focus on traditional European styles and one cider fermented naturally. On Vashon Island, Washington, Dragon's Head has experimented with natural fermentation, as has Virginia's Old Hill Hard Cider. These are specialty ciders, however—a way of experimenting with flavor and process in a cidery where pitching yeast remains the norm. This process is slow and expensive, but cider-makers will increasingly turn to it if there appears to be a market. In wine, beer, and spirits, super-premium artisanal products have found enthusiastic audiences.

So what is it about the traditional approach that appeals to Kevin? It's partly about the way the cider showcases the apple. Cider is an agricultural product, a beverage born on the tree. When you decant a bottle of Kevin's naturally carbonated, bubbly Cidre, he wants you to be able to smell and taste his apples. But I think there's something more to it than that. Even though they make cider differently in England, France, and Spain, the traditional makers I met all hinted at another reason they were willing to go to such effort. The less you do to a cider, the more you get out of it. When we were tasting his cider together, Kevin explained the flavors he was experiencing in the "front-palate, mid-palate, and back-palate"—and the descriptions through each phase were detailed and loving. If traditionalists could make the same cider in another way, they might be tempted. None of them—and this includes Kevin Zielinski—is convinced it's possible, however, so they do it the long, slow, old-fashioned way.

The Modernists

The Farnum Hill barn/cidery may have an organizing principle, but I couldn't detect it. A pod of wine barrels was basking in the sunshine near an open door, seemingly separated from the herd that huddled back in a dark room. Fermenters and tanks were tucked here and there, where they would accommodate the width of a forklift. In this way, it looked a whole lot like the cideries I had seen in Europe. One thing was different, though. Written on the barrels in chalk were these gnomic etchings: "Spitz," "Ash. K," "Wick." They were a clue that although Steve Wood considers his cider to be wholly authentic and natural, he does not subscribe to the traditionalist view.

"When we first started, we were trying to make English-style cider, thinking about French cider, and there really was a day we had an epiphany when we realized we were getting aromas and flavors that we never encountered [in Europe]. We slowly started to realize that a lot in England and France were kind of hidebound by tradition." Instead of European cider-makers, Steve turned to a different touchstone—American vintners. "We're basically trying to make wine with something else." Winemakers gave Farnum Hill the template it still uses to make its ciders, and this is a hallmark of this school of cider making.

When European cider-makers start bringing in their fruit, they don't pay special attention to the blend of apples. They look at the proportion of bitter, sweet, and acid apples, but work with the fruit that's available. A finished cider in France or England may use dozens of different varieties. Once the ciders have naturally fermented out, they might do a small amount of blending, but this is to adjust a gross element, like the level or type of acidity. That's not at all the approach at Farnum Hill, where the ciders are constructed very carefully to achieve a particular flavor profile.

The method of construction started from deconstruction: Early on, Steve and his team sat down to taste ciders and develop an objective vocabulary so they could identify what they were tasting. Steve said they told themselves, "If you smell peaches, dog shit, a frog, and dried apricots, that's what you write down." He doesn't like to mention this to his customers because it sounds fussy, but it was a key to not only understanding cider, but finding a way to describe what they were shooting for. They have detailed tasting notes going back years.

That's why there are casks bearing inscrutable chalk notations—they refer to cider made from particular apples (Esopus Spitzenburg, Ashmead's Kernel, and Wickson). They are all sharps, but "the difference between [them] is *huge*," Steve exclaimed. To illustrate, he took a small amount from each cask so I could taste them. It was striking. In one, the acidity was lacerating, just rough and vicious—it reminded me of some of the extreme sour beers American craft breweries make. Another was also sharply acidic, but it was bright and lemony and made you think of the rays of sunshine streaming into the cidery. Steve can use those different types of acidity to produce a flavor profile he likes. You can't un-blend cider, he pointed out ("it's like putting sugar in your coffee"), so the important blending at Farnum Hill happens before bottling.

"We're not thinking about the varietal mix—I mean, when we finally get something blended we'll reconstruct it [by variety]. We're not thinking about 42 percent Dabinett and 14 percent Wickson; we're thinking about what it smells and tastes like." In this way, Steve is able to use a specific palette to broadcast a Farnum Hill house flavor. "We're acid lovers," he told me. In England and France, some cider-makers want the softness that comes with malolactic fermentation, when the harsher malic acid is converted to gentler lactic acid, but Steve wants the edge of malic acid. With malolactic fermentations, "you get a peanut butter sandwich—absolutely no sharp acid left." Using the techniques gleaned from winemakers, he can put whatever edge on the cider he wants.

Another of the country's most respected cider-makers, Diane Flynt, has a similar approach. She's the founder of the Foggy Ridge cidery in the Blue Ridge Mountains of southwest Virginia. She did not start out, like Steve Wood, as an orchardist. She planted her trees specifically for cider making in 1997, focusing on some of the most illustrious of the old American cider apples: (Virginia's own) Hewe's Crab Apple, which by the time William Coxe was writing about it in 1817 was already at least one hundred years old, Harrison (Coxe: "produces a high coloured, rich and sweet cider of great strength"), Graniwinkle ("resembles a sirup in taste and consistency"), Newtown Pippin ("the finest apple of our country"), and several others. She grows more than thirty varieties, including some French and English apples. It wasn't until 2004 that she got her first full harvest, and the first Foggy Hill ciders came out the next year.

Wine is the reference point for Diane, too. When I asked her what she was trying to achieve with her ciders, she described her favorite wines. "High-elevation wines that have a lot of acidity, lower alcohol, very crisp, clean." In fact, she has hired a winemaker, Jocelyn Kuzelka, to help with the cider making. Foggy Ridge's orchards are up in the mountains at 3,000 feet [915 meters], far higher than those in Europe, New England, or the Pacific Northwest. At one point, she mentioned a fact other cideries have never highlighted: that a large diurnal variance (the difference between the day's high and low temperature) produced the best grapes—and, she felt, the best apples too. I sensed, as she was talking, that she was obliquely describing the Foggy Ridge palate when she talked about high-elevation fruit.

Diane has a rounded accent that makes it seem like she's speaking more slowly than she actually is. Continuing with the theme of making good ciders, she said, "We strive for a very clean ferment; I don't want a lot of funk." Like Steve, she's focused on the flavors of the apples. "We want to really express the fruit, because we go to a lot of trouble to grow the fruit." This is not an unusual perspective for an orchardist cider-maker. Orchardists spend a lot of time lovingly tending their trees and sampling their fruit. They have a proprietary sense over the flavor that they want drinkers to appreciate. But that's true of traditional cider-makers, too. For the modernists, though, even fermentation flavors occlude the apple.

PRODUCTION

There are times when it feels impossible to fully appreciate the variables that a cider-maker confronts. It seems that way to cider-makers, too. When he gets going, Steve Wood sounds like he has at least mapped the terrain of these variables, like booby traps he must carefully step around. In the course of one long burst of information, he touched on yeast strains, fermentation temperature, fermentation vessels, pH, and blending, and words like "mercaptans," "porosity," and "reductive aromas" rained down amid oblique references to the science of positive ions and binding sulfites. "We dump thousands of gallons of the stuff out on the ground because we tried something and it didn't work." He sighed. "It's possible to know more than somebody else about something and still know nothing."

He knows a lot. And more than that, what he has learned has given him pretty strong views about how to make cider. One of the defining characteristics of cider-makers like Steve is the use of yeast. Farnum Hill was fortunate to have the insight of Nicole LeGrand Leibon, who previously worked at White Labs, a yeast company. Steve has enormous respect for Nicole's palate, and she has been one of his key collaborators on blending. Despite all this sophistication, Farnum Hill uses a nearly fifty-year-old commercial strain, Pasteur Red Star Champagne yeast. After several yeast trials, "we decided we wanted something that ferments absolutely reliably to dryness and adds absolutely no character of its own." He chuckled and noted, "Wine guys hate that yeast because it doesn't do anything for you; we like it because it doesn't do anything for you." This view is the logical terminus of the get-yeast-out-of-the-way philosophy, but it typifies the modernist approach.

When I asked Diane Flynt about her yeast, I made the mistake of mentioning natural fermentation, and I think she must have thought I had a preference for it. "There's some romance about wild yeast, but wild yeast is *Saccharomyces*," she said when I stumbled into the question. (*Saccharomyces* is a strain of yeast, the same domestic or wild; she was in effect saying, "yeast is yeast.") "I think yeast *is* natural fermentation. There's not anything special about it. You can buy it; it's just *a* yeast." (For the record, I'm blissfully agnostic on the question of yeasts. I've enjoyed ciders made a multitude of ways.)

In fact, they think about yeast a lot at Foggy Ridge. The process there is to ferment different juices with different yeasts. "We choose yeast based on fermentation requirements, but also, we've found that some apples work better with some yeasts, with different yeasts than others." This went back to the process that both she and Steve use to construct their cider from blends. In the case of Foggy Ridge, though, Diane and Jocelyn believe different strains actually coax more of the character out of the fruit than purely neutral yeasts. A similar philosophy, but different approach.

Both ferment cold, and Diane uses stainless steel. ("We ferment like a winemaker.") Where Foggy Ridge uses multiple yeasts, at Farnum Hill, wood-aging helps develop character. Part of this has to do with the "porosity" of the oak that Steve mentioned earlier, but there's also "definite microbial interaction." I found this most curious: The yeast he wants perfectly neutral, but a *soupçon* of wood-borne bacteria he encourages. "Who *knows* what the hell is in there." He paused as he regarded the barrels. "We make a lot of gestures to the gods."

The most important—and most distinguishing—feature of this approach is blending. It's where the cider is actually put together, scent by scent, flavor by flavor. Both do a "field blend" of fruit coming in the door. This is to bring the acidity into a comfortably anti-microbial zone. "We're looking for a pH of like 3.5, *maybe* 3.6," Steve explained. "The Dabinett, for example, is like 4.4, so you need a lot of acid to bring that stuff down."

The final blends at both cideries result in product lines that have regular names, like Extra Dry, Farmhouse, and Semi-Dry (Farnum Hill) and First Fruit, Serious Cider, and Sweet Stayman. But like wine, these are vintage products and they taste different year to year. They have something recognizable, but it's impressionistic. When Steve was describing what he was shooting for with Extra Dry, he said, "We're looking for a bunch of the high fruits, little bits of tropical things, pineapple to grapefruit, orange and orange peel. We want the bitter and acid in pretty close balance with maybe the acid a little bit ahead of the bitter. We want the finish to carry the fruits all the way down and the acid to clean your palate."

I have spent some time in Oregon's Yamhill County drinking pinot noir and pinot gris, and I've spent time in Europe talking to traditional cider-makers. Not to put too fine a point on it, but Steve's description reminded me a lot more of the way vintners talk. That seems like a pretty good metaphor for the modernist cider-maker.

The Experimentalists

Evangelists come in all flavors, from the dogmatic, fire-and-brimstoners to the born-salesman P.T. Barnums. When Nat West decided to take his expansive home-cider operation pro in 2011, he made no bones about his preaching ambitions. He called his company Reverend Nat's and he speaks the gospel of cider to anyone who will listen. If you're looking for someone to sketch out (foresee?) what the future of American cider looks like, Nat is a pretty good place to start.

Reverend Nat's is a cidery of the modern variety, located in Portland, Oregon's dense inner Northeast on a surprisingly secluded, leafy side street. There are many trees about, but they grow from little bare patches cut out from the sidewalks. If there are any apple trees among the maples and oaks, they're ornamental species. The building is an old warehouse, but Nat has installed a cozy taproom near the entrance. When you walk in and sit down at the bar—as I did the first time I visited—your view is the cidery beyond. In the middle-distance are stacks of "totes"—plastic cubes the size of an industrial washing machine—bubbling with fermenting cider or sweating with thawing juice, while in the back of the cavern are large steel fermenters, adding depth to the visual tableau. The day I visited, one of Nat's assistants was filling carboys with juice for use in yeast trials.

Unless you're a close watcher of the burgeoning cider market, you're probably unaware of the nearly existential war taking place in the United States to define what cider should be. The protagonists in this battle run the gamut from the large industrial cideries who want you to think of cider as a sweet, appley frolic to artisanal producers like Steve Wood and Kevin Zielinski making sophisticated, complex products. Tentative new drinkers are caught in the middle, susceptible to the notion that there really is an answer to what cider "should" taste like.

Nat West is the perfect guy to reframe the discussion. He does not see the debate in terms of "sides." There is no cider-maker less doctrinaire, less driven by standards and tradition (which is just one clue that "Reverend Nat" and Nat West are not the same being). In the short time he has been making cider, Nat has been known for his flights of fancy. The cidery's flagship is called Hallelujah Hopricot, and is made to resemble a Belgian witbier (sort of). Nat spices the cider with coriander, bitter orange peel, and grains of paradise, infuses it with Cascade hops, and tops it off with apricot juice. Another of his potions includes ginger, lemongrass, lime zest, and wild quinine.

Kevin Zielinski uses natural fermentation for the same reason Steve Wood pitches an extremely neutral yeast—to accentuate the apple. Nat takes the opposite view. He uses beer yeasts to create more flavor for his ciders. The Hopricot uses a Belgian saison yeast famous for producing compounds that taste like tropical fruit. He also uses an English ale yeast and a Czech lager yeast. In each case, he chooses the yeast because of the flavors it adds to his cider, which from the traditionalist's perspective means obscuring the fruit.

At the same time, Nat is a student of cider making—he loaned me an American cider-making book from 1822—and produces wholly

Hopped Cider

Among the dense thicket of experimental American ciders, at least one group has emerged as a kind of modern-day standard: hopped cider. The first cidery to make one was, appropriately, Oregon's Wandering Aengus. More than 90 percent of the commercial hops produced in the United States are grown in Oregon and Washington, and Wandering Aengus is just a few miles from the nearest fields. "We got the ball rolling," said founder Nick Gunn, who credits his partner, James Kohn, with the idea, "and now there are a lot of hop ciders out there."

Because American cideries have to work with apples originally cultivated for eating, they regularly add in ingredients to round out the flavor profile. In beer, hops are boiled to convert certain acids into bittering compounds that help balance the sweetness of the malt. Cider isn't boiled, though, so the hops go into finished cider at cool temperatures. In brewing, this is called "dry-hopping," and brewers employ it to add aroma to their beer. That's how it works in cider, too, but because aroma is the central component in what we call "flavor," the bright, citrusy aromas seem to translate into taste as well as scent. Different hop varieties produce different aromas, so cideries can customize the flavor for their ciders.

Hopping a cider seems to create a bridge to beer drinkers, as well, especially on the West Coast, where hoppy beers are wildly popular. They provide an access point for beer drinkers, who find something recognizable in their local cider. It's difficult to track their numbers, but one can safely say there are dozens of hopped ciders on the market, and new ones arrive every month.

traditional products like a still Kingston Black English-style cider. He's one of the few American cider-makers to experiment with natural fermentation, and secretes bottles of English farmhouse cider behind the bar. One of his regular products is Revival Dry (which uses English bittersweets) and another is Newtown Pippin (made solely with the ancient American heirloom variety). Usually "experimental" refers to people doing things that deviate from the standards. With Nat, everything is grist for experimentation. After the 2013 harvest, he used the spent pomace from English bittersweet apples to make a naturally fermented ciderkin—a product he read about in the nineteenth-century book he loaned me.

Nat got his start as a home cider-maker, as a way of helping a friend get rid of his annual burden of backyard apples. He had been doing a project on his house and happened to have some twenty-ton house jacks handy. "So I whipped together a twenty-ton hydraulic cider press." He tells the story of what came next in suitably reverential tones. "I remember the first thing I did. It was summertime, so it was getting dark, and I had just finished getting it all together. I took the apple, put it in a metal bowl, and put the press on top of it and crushed the apple. Some juice came out and I shared some with my daughter and we drank it and we were like, 'Yes! This is awesome.'"

Nat started sharing his cider with friends at a regular potluck dinner he hosted every week, and his production grew and grew. Pretty soon he was scanning the neighborhood for trees he could use to feed his hobby. At one point he was making five hundred gallons of the stuff a year—the equivalent of thirty-two beer kegs. It was around that time that he found a small orchard that had cider fruit—bittersweets and heirloom apples. The regular production was spoken for, but Nat made a deal to buy the "windfalls"—those apples that fell to the ground in the autumn. From there, it wasn't a huge leap to convert it to a commercial operation.

PRODUCTION

Nat West and Reverend Nat are not the same person. The latter figure is an invention of the cidery—Colonel Sanders, not Martha Stewart. Yet West, with his long, old-timey goatee, sometimes seems a bit Reverendish. As we were touring the cidery, his way of speaking was mostly casual and almost folksy, and I imagine that at public events, he slides into the Reverend role easily enough. There were moments when he would drop paragraphs of dense technical explanations into conversation, though, and the portrait shifted. A question about fermentation sparked a comment about long-chain acids and sugar molecules. He gave me a more technical description of malolactic fermentation than I received anywhere else. And once, in describing bacteriological behavior, he veered from the scientific back to the folksy and amusing. "We get molds that are crazy—you get these fronds that are sticking straight up in the air. We have a fish-fry scooper and we just scoop it off the top."

He has a similarly dichotomous approach to making cider. On the one hand, the way he makes cider is purely modern America. Since it has been centuries since America made cider on a commercial scale, nearly all the apples have been bred for eating or cooking. In the Midwest and especially in New England some of the cooking varieties—Cortland, Newtown Pippin, Northern Spy—work pretty well in ciders. They don't have tannin, but they have aromatics, flavor, and acid.

In the Pacific Northwest, supermarket eating apples are king. Most of these varieties are bred for sweetness. Washington state produces 60 percent of the country's apples, and nearly 90 percent of those are just five varieties: Red Delicious, Gala, Fuji, Granny Smith, and Golden Delicious. Those apples are not particularly good for cider—in fact, they're bad—but they are *cheap*. Oregon cider-makers can have a 5,500-gallon truck of apple juice for no more than $2.20 a gallon. It's why the large majority of West Coast cideries just use dessert fruit. But lest you think a lesser apple makes a lesser cider, Nat would like a word with you.

"One of our company's unofficial mottos is 'making good cider out of bad apples.' Literally bad apples—they're not good apples." But, he says, "We're certainly not doing ourselves any favors by complaining about the lack of bittersweet apples. I'm like, Do you people have no imagination? Can we not figure out a way to make good-selling, honest cider with what we have on hand?"

Nat, of course, has no doubt about the answer to the question.

Cideries working with dessert fruit don't spend a lot of time fooling around with fermentation. I was surprised when I visited Wandering Aengus to find no conditioning tanks, just fermenters. Because the juice is largely just simple sugars, a dash of acidity, and very little in the way of interesting flavors or aromatics, there's no reason not to ferment a batch out fast. Nat can completely ferment his Hallelujah Hopricot in just six days. This is why he puts so much emphasis on yeast; since the fruit contributes so little, he leans on the yeast for added character. If he's using a beer yeast, he'll ferment it at the temperature appropriate to the type of beer—warm for his saison and English ale yeasts, cold for the lager strain. "We try to hit a taste; we pick a yeast for a taste and then we baby that yeast to get the most flavors out of it. We're aiming for esters, and we get more esters out of the hot stuff."

It's also why cideries regularly add spices, other fruit, and hops. I recently went to Bushwhacker's, the cider pub in Portland, to assemble a list of the extra ingredients appearing in American ciders on the store's shelves. What follows is not exhaustive, but it is more than a little suggestive: allspice, apricot, Asian pear, blackberry, boysenberry, brown sugar, caramel, cherry, chipotle, cinnamon, cloves, cucumber, currant, elderflower, gin-barrel, ginger, habanero,

The Sound of History Rhyming

Adding flavors to cider may strike you as the kind of thing that would only happen in these modern, debased times. In fact, humans were adding flavor at least two hundred years ago. Writing in 1822, James Thacher made the observation, "An English writer says that an infusion of hops is useful in cider, to give it a flavor, and an agreeable bitter. Another recommends grinding elderberries with the fruit, which gives the cider a fine color as well as flavor. . . . Ginger, cinnamon, spices, raisins, etc. have their advocates, who assure us that they are very good ingredients in cider." He went on to write the following, which I strongly believe are practices that will stay confined to the nineteenth century. "Some advise to make use of bullock's blood, calf's feet jelly, isinglass, etc. which may be well if the cider needs *doctoring*" (Thacher's emphasis). Even Nat West isn't likely to make a calf's-feet-jelly cider anytime soon.

honey, hops, juniper, lavender, raisins, raspberry, rose hip, smoked apple, tea, and verbena. I've tried enough of these to know that they're not all successful. The most interesting additives are subtle and evocative. They pick up a flavor or aroma latent in the cider and accentuate it. From time to time a bold flavor functions like an infusion, but then the drink becomes less like a cider and more like a cocktail.

In most of Nat's ciders, there's a blend of different ingredients and techniques, and this is another way to inflect a cider without overwhelming it. One of his most interesting projects involves fermenting apple and cherry juice with a strain of pure *Lactobacillus*. "Lacto" is the bacteria that turns milk into yogurt, and it is used in certain types of beer to produce a similar tangy flavor. It works surprisingly well with fruit juice, too, giving it a blast of acid, but also some softer esters that accentuate the juice. Amazingly, he pitched the bacteria at 95°F [35°C], and yet it was still free of the objectionable compounds bacteria sometimes produce.

We could go on and on—I'm not even going near Tepache, a Mexican pineapple cider—but one other cider deserves a mention. Nat has been conducting experiments in ciderkin, a very old cider that farmers used to make to extend their production. No matter how efficient a cider press is, the apple never releases all of its juice. Two hundred years ago, farmers re-wetted the spent pomace (skins, dry pulp, and seeds), let it sit a couple days, and pressed again. They got a thin juice that would make a low-alcohol cider. Nat does the same thing, letting the juice ferment naturally. When he's working with dessert-fruit pomace, he often adds botanicals to enhance the flavor of the ciderkin. If he has pomace that includes tannic apples, as he did when working in collaboration with the Portland-based cidery Cider Riot, he adds nothing else. The Cider Riot collaboration was one of the most interesting American ciders I've tasted. It had the aroma of a Basque cider but not the intensity; it was light, tart, and very refreshing.

Of all the world's cider regions, none is as interesting in the second decade of the twenty-first century as the United States. As I've toured around, I've asked cider-makers what kind of ciders they think Americans will be drinking in a decade. This is something they think about deeply—their livelihoods depend on it. If you zoom out to the bird's-eye view, they all agree: The future is biased toward "good" cider. They look at what happened when good spirits, wine, and beer started becoming more common, and they expect the same thing to happen with ciders. But when you zoom in and ask what "good" cider is, the differences among the three schools come into focus.

Steve Wood thinks good cider will be defined by fruit. "You gotta start with something that smells good and then you have to keep delivering on the promise. Tannin, fruit, acid, and some kind of balance." Cider won't come into its own until we have the fruit to make it special. "Most of the ciders, the so-called 'craft' ciders, are being made from apples that nobody wants anymore."

Kevin Zielinski is also committed to good fruit, but for him, tradition is even more important. "We are now on a different stage, and the players, all with motivation and zeal for the craft, are beginning to understand the traditions we have inherited. I choose to echo the past, to understand in today's age of technology the craft of cider making with traditional fruit."

Nat West had the most radical answer—one that made me re-think the idea of "proper" cider. In his view, there's a cultural residue clinging to the idea that a cider must be made a particular way. "American cider should have an American taste to it. I'm not defining what an American taste is, but an American taste is *not* English, it is *not* French. If you're trying to create a style or a culture, don't use other existing styles as your reference point. Look at what you have on hand here, and what people here are already used to and accustomed to. *No one* is accustomed to drinking French and English cider."

This is an incredibly liberating point of view. My own personal tastes run to the traditional and simple. Having visited cideries in England, France, and Spain, I can now taste those countries in a glass of traditional cider. Sometimes I pick up a *sagardoa* or *cidre* from the market just so I can take a little vacation to a Basque or French orchard. But those countries don't have the patent on authentic. There's absolutely nothing that says American cider-makers must follow their practices. "Who says that's better, that that's desirable even?" Nat asked. "We can grow bittersweet apples here, we make ciders with bittersweet apples, but do we need to? We've got great apples here—it's still called cider."

You find a ton of different products on the shelves right now all bearing the name "cider"—sweet, carbonated supermarket ciders like Angry Orchard; sophisticated, vinous ciders like Farnum Hill's; traditional, natural ciders like EZ Orchard's; and wildly experimental ciders like Reverend Nat's. At the moment, people are very interested in cider and they're all selling. It's very likely, however, that Americans will develop preferences. It's easy to distinguish English, French, and Spanish ciders, because drinkers in those countries have particular preferences. We don't know what "American" cider will taste like in the future, but there's a very good chance one of these cideries is already making it.

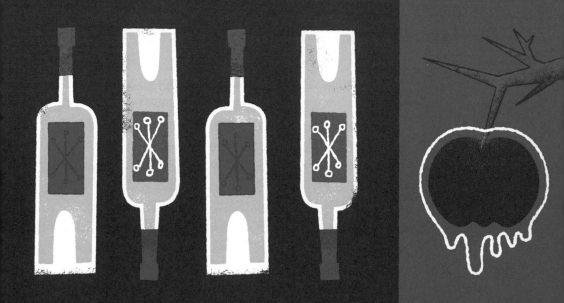

7 WINTER HARVEST IN QUEBEC

T here is no reason in the world that I can think of for why the terrain should change noticeably at the Vermont/ Quebec border, but it does. I have driven all over New England, from Providence up to Maine and over to Burlington, and the landscape looks much the same. The hills roll with rounded green slopes that burst open occasionally to expose outcroppings and walls of blocky pale granite. Open, deciduous forests fill the valleys, and nestled among them are frequent "sugar houses" where the famous maple syrup is made. Except for Boston and a few of the region's smaller cities, New England is very rural and, on the eastern side of the Green Mountains of Vermont, largely free of humans. Two highways run north-south on either side of the mountains, and the day I drove north from Hanover, New Hampshire, I encountered exactly nine cars before I reached the Canadian border. Along the way, the hills undulated, and I listened to a report from the local radio station on black bears. When I arrived at the international border, I was the only car in sight.

Once you pass into La Belle Province, however, the land flattens out. The trees become sparse or absent, and the sky seems to grow large, like Montana's. If you happen to be traveling around the countryside at the right time of year—November to January—you might chance upon a strange sight. There are certain species of apple trees in this region that don't release their fruit when the frost comes. The leaves they shed unsentimentally, but the branches clutch their apples—large, deep red spheres—which dangle like Christmas ornaments placed on the naked limbs of the wrong trees. As recently as twenty years ago, locals didn't pay a lot of attention to this odd phenomenon, until a man named Christian Barthomeuf had an idea.

Quebec's *Cidre de Glace*

They come in tall, narrow, clear-glass bottles, and they pour out like syrup. Forged from cold, these strange ciders are as unusual in flavor as appearance. During the long winter, cold concentrates the juice, and likewise the flavors, which explode on the tongue in vivid expressions of baked apple, icy shafts of tartness, and decadent layers of caramel sweetness. Ice ciders, or *cidre de glace*, are a surprisingly recent invention, a riff on the eisweins made by Quebecois just across the border from Vermont and New York. In less than two decades, they have become popular enough to support dozens of makers, and they are slowly entering the consciousness of drinkers unused to finding a new star in the cider universe.

Barthomeuf, a native of France who moved to Quebec in the 1970s, had been a struggling vintner. By the late 1980s, he was taking advantage of the most obvious feature of Quebec's terroir—its brutal winters—and making ice wines. At about the same time, he saw those strange apples in a neighbor's orchard and wondered if he could make an ice wine from apples. He conducted his early experiments on a noncommercial scale—he was a vintner, not an orchardist—but the results were promising. Those early experiments convinced him to postpone wine, and he began collaborating with cider-makers to produce the first commercial products. In 2002, he started his own cidery and winery (he still makes ice wines) called Clos Saragnat.

Ice wines were almost certainly discovered by accident, and the most common account dates to 1794. An early freeze snuck up on the winemakers of Franconia in Germany and turned their crop into beautiful little ice cubes. It's often described as a "frost," but it must have been more severe than that. The crop had to have been frozen solid, so much that the winemakers, out of desperation, decided to press the grapes as they were. Much of the liquid had turned to ice inside the grape; what trickled out of the press was a concentrated juice, the sugary liquid being more resistant to solid states. When fermented, it produced a heavy, rich wine prized for its intensity. The reason no one really remembers the origins of eiswein has to do with the climate of Germany. Early freezes were rare. Quebec, by contrast, is blessed with them and is, as a consequence, now the largest producer of ice wines. It is no wonder Canadians invented ice cider.

I was really keen to speak to M. Barthomeuf. When you write about fermented beverages, it is rare to have the chance to meet an actual inventor. The first cider-maker was dead before Christ was born. Even creators of modern devices like lightbulbs, cars, and telephones are long gone. Here was a living part of history, and I wanted to hear about the birth of the newest cider. I couldn't contact him before visiting Quebec, but I wasn't too worried—the website lists the dates and times the cidery is open to visitors. I had managed to schedule a tour with another pioneer of ice cider, Christian's first collaborator, François Pouliot, and I thought that would round out the historical lineage.

It was not to be. I dropped in one blustery late morning, as icy rain rattled on my windshield. It was early November, and as I pulled into Clos Saragnat's long driveway, I found myself circling one of the famous trees. It was laden with apples, but about half the leaves were gone—some fluttering down as I snapped pictures. Clos Saragnat is a beautiful cidery, and through an attractive little window, I spied sleek bottles of cider sitting on the counter. But the sign on the door said *fermé* (closed), and neither rapping vigorously at the door or sitting in my car another 45 minutes did me any good. There are plenty of articles detailing Barthomeuf's history, but I left Quebec without ever getting to experience his renowned ice ciders.

Fortunately, there are now dozens of Christian's artistic progeny in the area, and I learned the secrets of wintery cider making from François Pouliot, owner of La Face Cachée de la Pomme in Hemmingford, Quebec, as well as Eleanor Leger, who gave me an unscheduled tour of Eden Ice Cider on the American side of the border.

"Cooked" by Freezing

There are two ways to make ice cider, and the results are slightly different. The first way is the most romantic, which is also to say the most difficult. This is the method of collecting frozen fruit off trees and pressing during the darkest, iciest depths of winter. It is therefore the one least practiced. (Cider-makers use the fussy term "cryo-extraction," borrowed from ice-wine making, to describe it.) A much more common way is to press the fruit after harvest as you would any juice and then freeze that, rather than the apples. (It's given the equally fussy name "cryo-concentration.") The former is broadly considered to be the purest expression of ice cider, and it's the one Quebecois would like you to envision. (On travel sites and in cidery brochures, pictures of snow-topped apples are ubiquitous.) Only a small portion of the total ice-cider production is made this way, but it's hard to ignore its exotic allure.

When it's hanging on a tree, the apple is subject to severe conditions. The temperature dips, and the apple freezes. Ice crystals form and rupture the flesh of the fruit. The temperature rises and the apple thaws. Up and down the temperature goes, and inside the apple, the juice separates out. Pure water forms as ice in the center, and the sticky, heavy juice is forced outward toward the skin. When I arrived at La Face Cachée de la Pomme (literally "the hidden face of the apple"), François Pouliot was still engaged with a previous visitor, so an assistant gave me a tour of the cidery. She described what happens to the apple this way. "Because it's very sweet around in the flesh, it will stay a little bit soft. You can go into the orchard in January and bite into the apple. It's soft, *very* sweet. The taste of it when you bite into it is like a cooked apple coming out of the oven because it's cooked by the cold. The apple is a little bit brown, and soft, and crinkled."

The process is much harsher for the apple than for juice, and it creates unique compounds. I had visited the tasting room at Cidrerie Du Minot, just down the road from La Face Cachée in Hemmingford, the afternoon before I arrived, and my notes described it as "funky, musty, degraded, almost musky." When I got a chance to speak with François, he knew exactly the aroma I was describing. "Wild mushroom," he said, smiling. "When I first went to present it in France, this is what came out of the tasting. The customers were coming to taste, and they were referring to it as 'mushroom.' Here in North America you will never compare a wine to a mushroom because it's like an insult. But that's what it is. It's been twelve years, and I can't get it out of my mind." In his words, "It really gets more into the exotic fruit, rich—lychee, dry fig, apricot, banana. It's so exotic you can't even tell it's made from an apple."

François also intended to make wine before encountering ice cider. Indeed, he had already planted some vineyards, but lost the land on which they grew. While looking for a new piece of land, he found one with orchards and reasoned it would be good for grapes, too. But this is when he discovered the strange behavior of the winter fruit. His neighbor directed him to another farm where there were odd trees that didn't shed their bounty and he went to see them for himself. "So I went to see her around December and I said, 'Hello, Madame, I am Mister Pouliot. Would you mind if I go taste your apple?' She said, 'Are you crazy?'" The experience convinced him, though, and he leased her apples. There were only three varieties that produced winter fruit, and he took wood from those and grafted them back onto his own trees.

Since then, he has learned more about which varieties are best for freezing. Cortland apples will stay on the tree, but don't age well—the juice they produce isn't good for ice cider. The first orchard François visited had once been owned by a university that had made different hybrids, and one of those trees produced excellent winter-harvest fruit. François could find no name associated with the tree, so he named the apples that came off of it MacMillan and—of course—Pouliot. By this time, Christian Barthomeuf was selling small quantities of his own cider as *cidre doux*—"sweet cider," a term already used by the French for their very different keeved ciders. Together, Pouliot and Barthomeuf worked to produce the first commercial ice cider at La Face Cachée in 1994, which François re-christened *cidre de glace*.

The cidery at La Face Cachée is an award-winning structure built next to the 1842 stone home. Out front is a dense thicket of low-slung trees, and the lane winds through them on the way to the house. Since the industrial space was purpose-built for cider making, it has covered spaces that are uninsulated from the cold where apples can be pressed and juice frozen. Other areas *are* insulated, including a large room filled with bottles of slowly carbonating sparkling cider made in the French *méthode champenoise*. But this is just a side project. La Face Cachée is one of the two largest ice-cider producers, and François, whose ice ciders have accompanied meals at the White House, would like it to be recognized as one of the great (if recent) traditions in cider making.

"All the approaches we have," he said "we treat it as a wine."

Refrigeration Prohibited

Eden Ice Cider is located on a latitude just ten miles south of Clos Saragnat, and yet it is in a very key way on the wrong side of the tracks. The national border that separates the two cideries also separates Eden from a legal definition that protects ice cider in Quebec (not an appellation, but in the ballpark) as well as the national identity attached to *cidre de glace*. But even more important, there's a psychological line separating the countries. When I was sampling cider at Minot, the server was shocked that they had the climate to make ice cider in Vermont. "It's not cold enough, is it?" In the imagination of Canadians, *cidre de glace* can only be made in the snow and frost of their home country.

Americans, however, think of Vermont as plenty icy. Eden snuggles up to the border, close enough that as I was getting out of my car, I received a text message from AT&T welcoming me to Canada (new roaming rates apply!). The Eden cidery is on the farm of Albert and Eleanor Leger, an address in "West Charleston"—a town that doesn't seem to exist. (In rural England, addresses don't include streets or numbers; in the United States, they apparently sometimes include phantom towns.) Getting there takes you past Lake Willoughby, a spectacular, 300-foot glacier lake the color of clear winter sky, and you know you're getting close when you start passing orchards. The Legers founded the company in 2007 after a trip earlier to—where else?—Quebec. They wondered why no one was making ice cider in the States and decided to shoulder the responsibility themselves.

The Legers have been busy planting trees, originally in thirty-two varieties, but relying mainly on twelve. The bulk of their fruit, at least until their own trees mature, comes from other orchards, though. They have not made an emphasis of growing trees that produce winter apples, and instead press and freeze the juice. Eleanor was more concerned with the flavors of the different varieties, rather than their predilection for clinging to frozen branches. They actually experimented by storing the fruit until it froze, trying to replicate the process of cryo-extraction, but didn't like the results. "We got decomposition happening," she explained. "When you think about what happens when you freeze a lettuce leaf in your refrigerator-freezer? It doesn't come back."

Quebec, like New England, is an old apple-growing region, but the fruit was grown for eating. Some cultivars have acidity, especially the wild varieties, but the fruit was never planted to make cider. Eden does use old American and English cider varieties—Roxbury Russet, Ashmead's Kernel, St. Edmund's Russet, Esopus Spitzenburg—though mainly sharps, not varieties with high tannins. A key to a successful ice cider (on both sides of the border) is acidity. When the juice freezes, it concentrates not only the cider's sweetness, but its tartness. "It's all about balance," Eleanor said. "What's made ours successful is the balance."

The process sounds easy enough. Once they juice the apples, Eden puts them in cube-shaped plastic containers and stacks them on a concrete slab outside. This was a surprise to me—it seemed like artificial freezing would be more efficient. Eleanor corrected me. "You get a much more intense concentrate than if you were to put it in a commercial freezer; the juice is stuck in the matrix of the water. Even if you melt it, you don't get the yield and you don't get the concentrate." In this way, it's much the same as the process of freezing apples on the stem—with a natural climate, you get temperature variations, freezing, thawing, and eventually the concentrate comes to the bottom of the container through gravity. I would later learn that freezing the cider artificially is actually against the rules in Quebec—it must be done by Mother Nature.

Albert is a chemist, and through trial and error, they discovered that when it's 22°F [-6°C] inside the cube, "the stuff that's liquid—and there is stuff that's liquid at that temperature—is the right sugar level we're looking for."

Let's stop for a moment and consider that "stuff that's liquid." When a cider-maker presses an apple in the regular fashion, what trickles out is a liquid with a "brix" of about 12 percent sugar (brix is the measurement of sugar in a liquid solution). Eden subscribes to the Quebec rules governing ice cider, and they specify that the concentrated juice must have a *minimum* of 30 percent sugar. "It's a very cold, sticky job."

In fermented beverages, the amount of available sugar corresponds to the potential alcohol strength—but only to a point. The juice ice cideries start with is so sugary that the yeasts can't convert it all. Eden uses a Riesling strain and ferment at the warmish temperatures of 55 to 60°F [13 to 16°C]. They might be able to ferment it as strong as 14 percent or so before the environment became too alcoholic for the yeast to live, but they stop it at 10 percent, which is fairly typical for an ice cider. They drop the temperature back down to 35°F [2°C] and rack it twice, and all the yeast falls out. What they're left with at that point is a solution that *still* has a residual sugar of 19 percent—about 50 percent more sweet than regular apple juice. If they could somehow separate the alcohol from the unfermented juice, Eden would have enough sugar left to make a very strong cider.

According to François Pouliot, it takes eighty apples to make one 375-ml bottle of ice cider. The process takes months, or sometimes years, and requires a climate that has extended temperatures well below freezing. It is not a product for mass production—or mass consumption, for that matter. To accentuate this point, cider-makers have taken to using the bottles of ice wines—tall and narrow. One pours ice cider into cordials and sips them slowly, contemplatively. "It's not something you drink every day," said Eleanor. "It's for special occasions."

At the moment, if you live in a large city, you might find a bottle from Eden, La Face Cachée de la Pomme, or Pinnacle, but only if the gods of cider smile upon you. More likely, you'll only find them in their home region. The supply is low, and few Canadian companies export to the United States.

I brought back bottles from La Face Cachée de la Pomme and Cidrerie Du Minot (fortunately Eden *can* be found in Oregon) and shared them with some local cider-makers and cider fans. They were all impressed and intrigued. Ice ciders have flavors and characteristics present nowhere else in the cider world.

This is how, in the two short decades of their lives, *cidres de glace* have established themselves as a regional specialty. We can't speak of national tradition (perhaps the trends will turn against them), but there's every reason to believe that more and more producers will emerge and more of this rare and extraordinary beverage will make it to the tables of regular folk. In the coming decades, cider-makers will learn more about the best apples and methods to make these beverages. It's not every day we get to see the birth of a new tradition, and there's every reason to think that's what's happening in the flat, big-sky country of southern Quebec.

SOURCES

Books

Alwood, William B. *A Study of Cider Making*, Washington, D.C.: U.S. Department of Agriculture. 1903.

Brown, Pete, and Bill Bradshaw. *World's Best Ciders*, New York: Sterling Epicure. 2013.

Bruning, Ted. *Golden Fire: The Story of Cider*, London: New Generation Publishing. 2012.

Buell, J. S. *The Cider-Makers' Manual*, Buffalo: Haas and Kelly. 1869.

Cato the Elder. *De Agricultura*, translation by the Loeb Classical Library, rev. ed. Cambridge, Mass.: Harvard University Press. 1934.

Coxe, William. *A View of the Cultivation of Fruit Trees*, M. Carey and Son. 1817.

Hawthorne, Nathaniel. *The Marble Faun* (1860). New York: Penguin Classics. 1990.

Janik, Erika. *Apple: A Global History*, London: Reaktion Books. 2011.

Kurlansky, Mark. *The Basque History of the World*, London: Walker. 1999.

Lea, Andrew, and John Piggott, eds. *Fermented Beverage Production*, 2nd ed, New York: Kluwer Academic/Plenum Publishers. 2003.

Proulx, Annie. *Making the Best Apple Cider*, North Adams, Mass.: Storey Publishing. 1980.

Quinion, Michael B. *Cidermaking*, Oxford: Shire Publications. 1982.

Thacher, James. *The American Orchardist*, 2nd ed., Ezra Collier. 1825.

Watson, Ben. *Cider, Hard and Sweet*, 2nd ed., Woodstock, Vt.: Countryman Press. 2009.

Articles

Cornille, Amandine, et al. "New Insight into the History of Domesticated Apple: Secondary Contribution of the European Wild Apple to the Genome of Cultivated Varieties." *PLoS Genetics*. 2012.

Del Campo, Gloria, et al. "Development of Alcoholic and Malolactic Fermentations in Highly Acidic and Phenolic Apple Musts." *Bioresource Technology* 99. 2008.

Nabhan, Gary Paul. "The Fatherland of Apples." *Orion Magazine* May/June. 2008.

Todd, Cain. "Expression and Objectivity in the Case of Wine: Defending the Aesthetic Terroir of Tastes and Smells." *Rivista di Estetica* 51. 2012.

Website

Lea, Andrew. "Wittenham Hill Cider Pages." 1997 onward. Cider.org.uk/frameset.htm.

Tours and Interviews

ENGLAND
Chris Hecks. Hecks Farmhouse Cider. Tour, January 21, 2014.
Mike Johnson. Ross-on-Wye Cider and Perry. Tour, January 19, 2014.
Tom Oliver. Oliver's Cider and Perry. Tour, January 20, 2014.

FRANCE
Guillaume Drouin. Calvados Christian Drouin. Tour, January 24, 2014.
Cyril Zangs. Cyril Zangs Cidery. Tour, January 23, 2014.

QUEBEC
Cidrerie du Minot. Visit, October 31, 2013.
François Pouliot. La Face Cachée de la Pomme. Tour, October 31, 2013.

SPAIN
Miguel Mari (translator: Ainhoa Lobedegi). Isastegi. Tour, January 29, 2014.
Ainize Mitxelena. Basque Cider Museum. Tour, January 28, 2014.
Javier Quintero. Sarasola. Tour, January 27, 2014.

UNITED STATES
Diane Flynt. Foggy Ridge Cider. Phone interview, April 14, 2014.
Nick Gun and James Kohn. Wandering Aengus. Tour, September 20, 2013.
Greg Hall. Virtue Cider. Interview, June 23, 2013.
Josh Johnson. Finnegan Cider. Tour, October 17, 2013.
Eleanor Leger. Eden Ice Cider. Tour, October 29, 2013.
Morgan Miller. Interview, February 24, 2014.
David Sipes. Angry Orchard. E-mail interview, March 28, 2014.
Nat West. Reverend Nat's. Tour, October 10, 2014.
Steve Wood. Farnum Hill Ciders. Tour, October 28, 2013.
Kevin Zielinski. EZ Orchards. Tour, September 26, 2013.

ACKNOWLEDGMENTS

It would have been impossible to write this book without the help of the cider-makers who spoke to me and gave me tours of their cideries. I never stop being surprised how patient, generous, and forthcoming cider-makers are. A few of them were kind enough to keep helping me, by offering insight and further information, over the course of the book-writing process: Nat West, Kevin Zielinski, and Tom Oliver. Morgan Miller, a long-time chronicler of the American cider scene, was another regular source of guidance. I offer you all my great thanks.

Although she does not make a formal appearance in the book, my wonderful wife, Sally, was along for the ride—and in the case of the European jaunt, literally. She was not only supportive of the project, but a valuable partner in sensory evaluation (I at least comfort myself in knowing that the research wasn't too onerous).

Finally, to Amy Treadwell of Chronicle Books—thanks so much for thinking of me. It was nice to write about something other than beer for a change.

INDEX

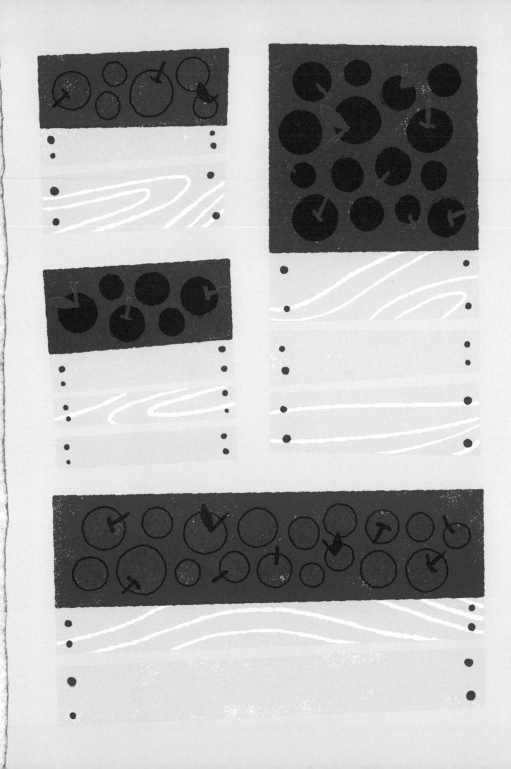